SEMIOTEXT(E) INTERVENTION SERIES

© Amsterdam, 2011. Published by arrangement with Agence litteraire Pierre Astier & Associés.
This translation © 2012 by Semiotext(e)

Cet ouvrage publié dans le cadre du programme d'aide à la publication bénéficie du soutien du Ministère des Affaires Etrangères et du Service Culturel de l'Ambassade de France représenté aux Etats-Unis.

This work received support from the French Ministry of Foreign Affairs and the Cultural Services of the French Embassy in the United States through their publishing assistance program.

Published by Semiotext(e)
PO Box 629, South Pasadena, CA 91031
www.semiotexte.com

Thanks to John Ebert.

Design: Hedi El Kholti
Inside cover photograph: Michael Oblowitz

ISBN: 978-1-58435-115-3
Distributed by The MIT Press, Cambridge, Mass.
and London, England
Printed in the United States of America

10 9 8 7 6 5 4

Maurizio Lazzarato

The Making of

the Indebted Man

An Essay on the Neoliberal Condition

Translated by Joshua David Jordan

semiotext(e)
intervention
series □ 13

Contents

Foreword

As it has in other regions of the world, the class struggle is today unfolding and intensifying in Europe around the issue of debt. The debt crisis has struck the United States and the UK, that is, those countries in which the latest financial catastrophe and, more important, neoliberalism itself originated.

The debtor-creditor relationship—the subject of this book—intensifies mechanisms of exploitation and domination at every level of society, for within it no distinction exists between workers and the unemployed, consumers and producers, working and non-working populations, retirees and welfare recipients. Everyone is a "debtor," accountable to and guilty before capital. Capital has become the Great Creditor, the Universal Creditor. As the current "crisis" leaves no room to doubt, property remains one of the major political stakes of neoliberalism, since the creditor-debtor relationship is a product of power relations between owners (of capital) and non-owners (of capital).

Through public debt entire societies become indebted. Instead of preventing "inequalities," the latter exacerbates them. It is high time we call these inequalities, simply, "class differences."

The economic and political illusions of the last forty years have one by one fallen away, rendering neoliberal policies all the more brutal. The "new economy," the information and knowledge societies, have all been absorbed by the debt economy. In those democracies that triumphed over communism, just a handful of people (certain functionaries at the IMF, the European Central Bank, the EU, and a few politicians) now decide for everyone according to the interests of a minority. The debt economy has deprived the immense majority of Europeans of political power, which had already been diminished through the concessions of representative democracy. It has deprived them of a growing share of the wealth that past struggles had wrested from capitalist accumulation. And, above all, it has deprived them of the future, that is, of time, time as decision-making, choice, and possibility.

The series of financial crises has violently revealed a subjective figure that, while already present, now occupies the entirety of public space: the "indebted man." The subjective achievements neoliberalism had promised ("everyone a shareholder, everyone an owner, everyone an entrepreneur") have plunged us into the existential condition of the indebted man, at once responsible and guilty for his particular fate. The present essay offers an exploration and genealogy of the economic and subjective production of indebted man.

Since the last financial crisis following the dot-com bust, capitalism has abandoned the epic narratives it had constructed around the "conceptual types" of the entrepreneur, the creative visionary, and the independent worker, "proud of being his own boss." By pursuing their personal interests alone, these types supposedly work for the good of all. The dedication, subjective motivation, and the *work on the self* preached by management since the 1980s have become an injunction to *take upon oneself* the costs and risks of the economic and financial disaster. The population must take charge of everything business and the Welfare State "externalize" onto society, debt first of all.

According to business leaders, the media, politicians, and experts, the causes of the current situation are not to be found in the fiscal and monetary policies that have deepened deficits and transferred enormous wealth to business and the rich. Nor are they to be found in the series of financial crises which, after having all but vanished in the immediate postwar period, are now recurrent, leading to the extortion of enormous amounts of money from the population to avoid a so-called "systemic" crisis. For all these amnesiacs, the true causes of the repeated crises lie in the excessive demands of the governed (especially those of Southern Europe), who want nothing more than to laze about, and in the corruption of the elites, who, in reality, have always had a hand in the international division of labor and power.

The neoliberal power bloc cannot and does not want to "regulate" the "excesses" of finance because its political program continues to be based on the choices and decisions that brought us the latest crisis. Instead, with its threat of sovereign debt default, it seeks to follow through on a program it has been fantasizing about since the 1970s: reduce wages to a minimum, cut social services so that the Welfare State is made to serve its new "beneficiaries"—business and the rich—and privatize everything.

We lack the theoretical tools, concepts, and vocabulary that would allow us to analyze not only finance but the economy of debt, which at once encompasses and goes beyond finance and its politics of subjection.

In the present book, we are going to draw on Deleuze and Guattari's return to the creditor-debtor relation in *Anti-Oedipus*. Published in 1972, it anticipates at a theoretical level the shift

Capital would later make in fact. Through our readings of Nietzsche's *Genealogy of Morality* and Marx's theory of money, it will help us revive two hypotheses. The first, that the paradigm of the social lies not in exchange (economic and/or symbolic) but in credit. There is no equality (of exchange) underlying social relations, but rather an asymmetry of debt/credit, which precedes, historically and theoretically, that of production and wage labor. The second hypothesis, that debt represents an economic relationship inseparable from the production of the debtor subject and his "morality." The debt economy combines "work on the self" and labor, in its classical sense, such that "ethics" and economics function conjointly. The modern notion of "economy" covers both economic production and the production of subjectivity. Traditional categories rooted in 19th- and 20th-century revolutions—labor, society, and politics—are now informed and in large measure have been redefined by debt. It is therefore necessary to venture into enemy territory to analyze the debt economy and the production of indebted man in order to construct the theoretical weapons for the struggles to come. For far from ending, the crisis is more than likely to spread.

1

UNDERSTANDING DEBT AS
THE BASIS OF SOCIAL LIFE

This isn't a crisis, it's highway robbery.
—Protestors at Puerta del Sol

This isn't a rescue, it's a sell-off.
—A Greek union member

Credit brings us back to a situation characteristic of feudalism, in which a portion of labor is owed in advance, as serf labor, to the feudal lord.
—Jean Baudrillard, *The System of Objects*

On October 12, 2010, UNEDIC,[1] which collects unemployment taxes on wages and provides aid to the unemployed as well as to precarious and seasonal workers, etc., published the following press release:

UNEDIC is pleased to announce that its long- and short-term ratings have been issued by three ratings agencies, Fitch (AAA/F1+), Moody's (AAA/P-1), and Standard & Poors (AAA/A-1+). The ratings review began following the meeting of the board of directors on July 29 and ended on October 8, 2010. The excellent ratings will allow UNEDIC to carry out its financing plan and therefore guarantee continuity in the payment of unemployment benefits. On September 10, 2010, the latest technical budget forecast for unemployment insurance showed UNEDIC's total debt approaching 13 billion euros by December 2011.

How is it that ratings activity and trading operations carried out in the plush offices of banks and investment institutions have an effect on unemployed, precarious, seasonal, occasional, and temporary workers?

Well, UNEDIC regularly posts deficits. First of all, because of the drop in revenue due mainly to tax breaks on employers (the French Treasury exempts 22 billion euros in employer contributions every year in the name of the government's "jobs policy"). Second, because taxes on precarious, occasional, and temporary labor cannot cover the costs of compensation. With the explosion of "precarious" work (short-term, occasional, seasonal, temporary) advantageous to business, the compensation system is now "structurally" in the red.

Rather than raising employer tax rates, UNEDIC—as any self-respecting business would—has borrowed money by issuing bonds on financial markets. In December 2009, it borrowed 4 billion euros, then 2 billion more in February 2010. Financial institutions rushed in to buy them and in less than an hour all the bonds had been sold. Investors' appetite is easy to understand, of course. International ratings agencies (the same that have given low ratings to Ireland, Greece, Portugal, and Spain, causing spikes in interest rates, effectively imposing austerity budgets on the countries; the same that gave top ratings to "toxic securities," the primary cause of the subprime crisis; the same that gave good grades to corporations guilty of embezzlement like Enron; the same that failed to see the latest financial crisis coming) have given, as the press release puts it, "excellent ratings" and a "guarantee" to investors.

Thus, in order to "save the system" of compensation from "default" (the threat is always the same), the logic of finance must be introduced into a private institution—although one serving the "public interest" like UNEDIC—with the following consequences:

1) The interest rate applied on the 6 billion euro loan is around 3%, which means that unemployment taxes have now become a new source of revenue for financial institutions, pension funds, and banks. If Moody's lowers its rating, as it has recently done for Ireland, Greece, and Portugal, UNEDIC's borrowing rate rises and then finance takes a still larger draw on tax revenue, which in turn decreases the availability of funds for welfare programs.

2) The three agencies' ratings inevitably weigh on negotiations over unemployment insurance accords, which determine the duration and amount of compensation for the following three years. In order to maintain good ratings, unions and employers must act in accordance with the demands of ratings agencies rather than with those of the unemployed, since interest is tied to the ratings.

3) Due to their "power of evaluation," the agencies have entered into managing unemployment insurance. The co-management of insurance, which had been guaranteed by unions and employer associations, has been opened to private investors who now have their word to say. Agencies' "evaluation" has become part of the general evaluation of the "health," "efficiency," and "profitability" of unemployment insurance. During protests in France involving intermittent workers as well as those of the unemployed in winter 1997/1998,

both groups attempted to break the union-employer duopoly in order to bring "precarious" workers poorly represented by unions into the management of unemployment insurance. The unions, however, think and act solely in the defense of full-time wage-earners' rights. The demand to make management over insurance coffers more democratic came to naught. Meanwhile, "industrial capitalists," insurance capitalists, and the State have quietly brought financial capitalists into the game.

All the terms of UNEDIC's loan are not known. We can only hope that the rates are less "usurious" than those agreed upon by local governments, which, unable to turn to the national government for aid, have had to turn to financial markets. The debt of French administrative regions and departments has risen 50% since 2001. One example among others: On February 9, 2011, the departmental government of Seine-Saint-Denis decided to sue three banks (Depfa, Calyon, Dexia) with which it had so-called toxic loans in order to have them invalidated. On January 1, 2011, Seine-Saint-Denis debt reached 952.7 million euros, 71.7% of which was toxic. In all, the department had subscribed to 63 toxic loans. The same financial products were sold to numerous other local governments. They were tied to highly volatile indexes with the potential for major hikes in interest payments. As an elected official put it to the press, "The initial rate, over three years, was 1.47%. It is now 24.20%, which comes to a jump of 1.5 million euros a year, nearly the cost of a daycare center."

The amounts from unemployment funds and local government revenue going to creditors make up only a tiny portion of the money drawn each year by international finance on the income of the national population.

In France, interest payments on national debt rose to 50 billion euros in 2007. It is the second highest item in the French budget after education and before defense. Each year it swallows up nearly all income tax revenue.[2]

The deepening national debt is one of the principal results of neoliberal policies, which have sought, since the mid-1970s, to transform the financing structure of Welfare-State spending. The most significant laws, then, adopted by every European government and included in various European treaties, have been those prohibiting central banks from coining money to ease public debt. Local governments, like all Welfare State services, can no longer be financed in this way but must instead appeal to "financial markets." This is what is called "Central Bank independence," which, translated into normal language, means in practice a dependence on markets, since these laws make it necessary to turn to private creditors and submit to the conditions dictated by shareholders, bondholders, and the other owners of securities. Before the laws, the State could seek interest-free financing through the central bank and pay its debt back as revenue came in. It has been estimated that interest payments on debt since 1974 (when the French government began having to seek market financing) total nearly 1.2 trillion euros out of a total 1.64 trillion in public debt. Debt interest reveals the extent to which markets have been able to plunder the population over the last forty years.

The "capture" of value also affects businesses. Neoliberal policies have transformed them into mere financial assets as they "pay more money to their shareholders than their shareholders pay out."[3]

Consumption, which makes up the largest share of GDP in developed countries (in the US it comes to 70%), is another major source of creditor "revenue." In the US, the largest family purchases (a house, a car and maintenance, education expenses) are made on credit. But consumption runs on debt even for everyday purchases, quite often paid for with a credit card. In the US and the UK, the level of household debt relative to disposable income is, respectively, 120% and 140%. The subprime crisis showed that credit card debt is part of the great mass of securitized credit (debt transformed into negotiable securities), along with real estate, automobile, and student loans.

Through consumption, we maintain an unwitting relationship with the debt economy. We carry within us the creditor-debtor relation—in our pockets and wallets, encoded in the magnetic strip on our credit cards. Indeed, this little strip of plastic hides two seemingly harmless operations: the *automatic* institution of the credit relation, which thereby establishes *permanent* debt. The credit card is the simplest way to transform its owner into a permanent debtor, an "indebted man" for life.[4]

WHY A DEBT ECONOMY AND NOT A FINANCE ECONOMY?

Through the simple mechanism of interest, colossal sums are transferred from the population, business, and the Welfare State to creditors. This is why Gabriel Ardent argued as early as the 1970s that the financial system, in the same way as the money and credit systems, is a "power mechanism of exploitation." The so-called "real" economy and business are but aspects of the capitalist process of valorization, accumulation, and exploitation: "On closer examination, the financial system is perhaps more oppressive."[5] Credit is "one of the most effective instruments of exploitation man has managed to create, since certain people, by producing credit, are able to appropriate the labor and wealth of others."[6] What the media calls "speculation" represents a machine for capturing and preying on surplus value in conditions created by modern-day capitalist accumulation, conditions in which it is impossible to distinguish rent from profit. The process coverting control over capital production and property, which began in Marx's time, is now complete. The "actually functioning capitalist," as Marx noted long ago, is transformed into "a mere manager, in charge of other people's capital," and "the capital owner"[7] into a financial capitalist or rentier. Finance, banks, and institutional investors are not mere speculators but the (representatives of) "owners" of capital, whereas those who were once "industrial capitalists," the entrepreneurs who risked their own capital, have been reduced to the "functionaries" ("wage-earners" or those paid in company stock) of financial valorization.

We must therefore remove all moral connotations from the notion of rent. The euthanasia of the rentier, his eviction from the economy, contrary to what Keynes had in mind, which was that it become the watchword of capitalist restructuring following the 1929 crisis, would not mean the euthanasia of "speculation" but of capitalism itself. It would mean the death of private property and patrimony, the two political mainstays of neoliberal economies. All of modern-day capitalist accumulation is, moreover, comparable to rent. The real estate market, the continual rise in housing prices, constitutes a kind of rent (and what rent it is, especially in the US!), in the same way we pay a rent for intellectual property each time we buy a product covered by copyright. Still, we should not get bogged down in mere denunciation.

Reducing finance to its speculative function neglects its political role as representative of "social capital" (Marx), which industrial capitalists will not and cannot concede, as well as its function as "collective capitalist" (Lenin), which, through governmental practices, bears on society as a whole. It also neglects the "productive" function of finance, its ability to make profits. The share of total corporate profits from American financial, insurance, and real estate companies nearly matched in the 1980s and exceeded in the 1990s the share from manufacturing. In England, finance is the leading sector of the economy.

Moreover, it is impossible to separate finance from production, since the former is an integral part of every sector of the economy. Finance, industry, and the tertiary sector work in symbiosis.

The automobile industry, to take but one example, functions entirely on credit mechanisms (loans, leasing, etc.). Consequently, General Motors' business is just as much automobile production as—and perhaps even more so—consumer credit, which is indispensable to the sales of its products to consumers. In other words, we are in an historic period in which finance is consubstantial with all types of production of goods and services.[8]

In neoliberalism, what we reductively call "finance" is indicative of the increasing force of the creditor-debtor relationship. Neoliberalism has pushed for the integration of monetary, banking, and financial systems by using techniques revelatory of its aim of making the creditor-debtor relationship a centerpiece of politics. For integration clearly reflects a power relation based on property. In the current crisis, the relation between owners (of capital) and non-owners (of capital) has expanded its hold over all other social relations.

One of these neoliberal techniques is "securitization."[9] Since the passage of a law sponsored by the Socialist Pierre Bérégovoy in 1988 in France, securitization has made it possible to transform debt into tradable securities on the financial market. What is called financialization represents less a form of investment financing[10] than an enormous mechanism for managing private and public debt and, therefore, the creditor-debtor relation, through methods of securitization. Consequently, rather than speak of finance, it is more accurate to speak of "debt" and "interest."

We do not intend here to analyze "finance," its internal mechanisms, the logic guiding traders' decisions, etc., but rather the relation between creditor and debtor. In other words, contrary to what economists, journalists, and other "experts" never tire of repeating, finance is not an excess of speculation that must be *regulated*, a simple capitalist function ensuring investment. Nor is it an expression of the *greed* and *rapaciousness* of "human nature" which must be rationally *mastered*. It is, rather, a power relation. Debt is finance from the point of view of the debtors who have to repay it. Interest is finance from the point of view of creditors, security-holders who guarantee they benefit from debt.

Politically, the *debt economy* seems to be a more appropriate term than finance or financialized economy, not to mention financial capitalism, since with it one can straightaway understand what is at stake: The debt that the Greeks, Irish, Portuguese, English, and Icelanders do not want to repay and against which they have been protesting over the last several months; the debt that legitimizes the increase in British university tuition and has provoked violent clashes in London; the debt that justifies cutting off 800 euros per family in the UK in order to reestablish a balanced budget in the aftermath of the financial crisis; the debt that calls for budget cuts in education in

Italy and which Roman students have risen up to oppose; the debt that cuts social services, financing of the arts, unemployment and basic welfare benefits in France and, with a new stability pact, in all of Europe.

Now that we have established that the current crises are not the result of some kind of uncoupling of finance and production, of the so-called "virtual" and the "real" economy, but are instead indicative of the balance of power between creditors and debtors, we shall now examine the growing hold of debt on neoliberal politics.

MANUFACTURING DEBT

Debt is not an impediment to growth. Indeed, it represents the economic and subjective engine of the modern-day economy. Debt creation, that is, the creation and development of the power relation between creditors and debtors, has been conceived and programmed as the strategic heart of neoliberal politics. If debt is indeed central to understanding, and thus combating, neoliberalism, it is because neoliberalism has, since its emergence, been founded on a logic of debt. One of the turning points in neoliberalism has thus been defined by what economists call the "shock" of 1979. The latter, by enabling the accumulation of enormous public deficits, opened the door to a debt economy and began the reversal of power relations between creditors and debtors. In 1979, on the urging of Paul Volker (head of the Federal Reserve at the time and economic advisor of the first Obama team), nominal rates (interest on debt reimbursement) more than doubled, rising from 9% to 20%, whereas over the preceding period they had on average trended downward. "These high rates created completely new cumulative State (public) or national (foreign) debt. The wealthy had thus constructed a mechanism for the extreme polarization of creditors and debtors on an unprecedented scale,"[11] which all went to the good of creditors.

The impossibility of doing anything about public, that is, State, debt through monetary mechanisms (recourse to the Central Bank) led to the expansion of financial markets, which have, once again, been enlisted, developed, and imposed at each step by the State. Furthermore, in France, most of the corresponding policies have been enacted by Socialist governments.

Financial markets have been structured and developed as part of the management of State debt since 1979 energy crisis. States have not stopped at opening up financial markets, however; they have assisted in establishing the organizations and structures needed for them to thrive.

They thus broadened (by diversifying the range of securities issued on primary markets) and deepened (by increasing transaction volume on secondary markets) the markets for public-sector securities that would attract investors. The yield curve for these securities has become the benchmark for asset pricing in lieu of the base rate.[12]

Monetary policies, wage-deflation policies, Welfare State policies (reductions in public spending), and fiscal policies (transfers of several points of GDP to corporations and the population's wealthiest in all industrialized countries) have come together to create enormous public and private debt. Debt reduction, which is now the order of the day in all countries, does not run counter to debt creation, since debt serves to prolong and expand the neoliberal political program. On the one hand, it means taking back control of "social issues" and Welfare State spending through austerity measures, that is, taking back control of revenue, time (of retirement, vacation, etc.), and the social services that have been wrested through social struggle from capitalist accumulation. This objective has been made explicit in the program of "Refounding Society" advanced by French employers, whose leadership, since the end of the last century, has gone from the hands of the bosses in metallurgy to those of insurers and financiers. With the program's announcement, its chief ideologue, Denis Kessler, argued that "economic imperatives" had once again to be brought to bear on "social issues, which at times have had too great a tendency to be taken separately or even dominate economic imperatives."[13] On the other hand, it means pursuing and expanding the process of privatization of Welfare State services, that is, transforming them into a sector for accumulation and profitability for private enterprise. The latter must "reinternalize" the social protections that it had externalized during Fordism by "delegating" them to the State. (Insurers especially, the new leaders of the French employer union [the Mouvement des Entreprises de France, MEDEF], feel that they were "robbed" in 1945.) The austerity plans the IMF and Europe have imposed on Greece and Portugal thus include "new privatizations." Reflecting on the measures, a Greece trade unionist remarked that, rather than a "rescue" plan, they represent no less than a "wholesale sell-off."

In this way, the debt economy brings with it a kind of capitalism in which the savings of workers and of the population in general, pension funds, public health insurance, and social services, "because administered in a world of competition, would once again become a function of business interests."[14] In 1999, Denis Kessler estimated at 2.6 trillion francs, or 150% of the State budget, the spoils social spending opened up to business. The privatization of social insurance mechanisms, the individualization of social policies, and the drive to make social protections a function of business constitute the foundations of the debt economy.

The power bloc of the debt economy has seized on the latest financial crisis as the perfect occasion to extend and deepen the logic of neoliberal politics.

A POWER RELATION SPECIFIC TO DEBT

Debt acts as a "capture," "predation," and "extraction" machine on the whole of society, as an instrument for macroeconomic prescription and management, and as a mechanism for income redistribution. It also functions as a mechanism for the production and "government" of collective and individual subjectivities. In order to account for the new functions of finance, André Orléan's heterodox economic theory speaks of "creditor power" and "debt power," whose force "can be measured by the ability to transform money into debt and debt into property and, in so doing, to directly influence the social relations that structure Western society."[15] Orléan defines the creditor-debtor relation as the mainspring of the transformation of capitalist "governance" (a term from the neolanguage of power meaning "command"): "We have moved from Fordist regulation, which privileged the industrial and debtor side, to financial regulation, which prioritizes the financial and creditor side."[16]

But the creditor-debtor relation does more than "directly influence social relations," since it is itself a power relation, one of the most important and universal of modern-day capitalism. Credit or debt and their creditor-debtor relationship constitute specific relations of power that entail specific forms of production and control of subjectivity—a particular form of *homo economicus*, the "indebted man." The creditor-debtor relationship encompasses capital/labor, Welfare-State services/users, and business/consumer relations, just as it cuts through them, instituting users, workers, and consumers as "debtors."

Debt produces a specific "morality," at once different from and complementary to that of "labor." The couple "effort-reward" of the ideology of work is doubled by the morality of the *promise* (to honor one's debt) and the *fault* (of having entered into it). As Nietzsche reminds us, the concept of "Schuld" (guilt), a concept central to morality, is derived from the very concrete notion of "Schulden" (debts). The "morality" of debt results in the moralization of the unemployed, the "assisted," the users of public services, as well as of entire populations. The German press campaign against Greek parasites and loafers bears witness to the violence of the guilt engendered by the debt economy. When it comes to talking about debt, the media, politicians, and economists have only one message to communicate: "You are at fault," "You are guilty." The Greeks laze about in the sun while German Protestants slave away under gloomy skies for the good of Europe and humanity.

The power of debt is described as if it were exercised neither through repression nor through ideology. The debtor is "free," but his actions, his behavior, are confined to the limits defined by the debt he has entered into. The same is true as much for the individual as for a population or social group. You are free insofar as you assume the *way of life* (consumption, work, public spending, taxes, etc.) compatible with reimbursement. The techniques used to condition individuals to live with debt begin very early on, even before entry on the job market.[17] The creditor's power over the debtor very much resembles Foucault's last definition of power: an action carried out on another action, an action that keeps the person over which power is exercised "free." The power of debt leaves you free, and it encourages you and pushes you to act in such a way that you are able to honor your debts (even if, like the IMF, it has a tendency to devour "debtors" by imposing economic policies that promote "recession").

Neoliberalism governs through multiple power relations: creditor-debtor, capital-labor, welfare programs-user, consumer-business, etc. But debt is a universal power relation, since everyone is included within it. Even those too poor to have access to credit must pay interest to creditors through the reimbursement of public debt; even countries too poor for a Welfare State must repay their debts.

The creditor-debtor relation concerns the entirety of the current population as well as the population to come. Economists tell us that every French child is born 22,000 euros in debt. We are no longer the inheritors of original sin but rather of the debt of preceding generations. "Indebted man" is subject to a creditor-debtor power relation accompanying him throughout his life, from birth to death. If in times past we were indebted to the community, to the gods, to our ancestors, we are henceforth indebted to the "god" Capital.

We currently lack the theoretical tools to analyze the entire scope of the relation of power between creditor and debtor and the different functions of debt. The concept of speculation only covers one aspect of how debt works and prevents us from seeing how it produces, distributes, captures, and shapes subjectivity.

We are therefore going to return to Deleuze and Guattari's work, which was always faithful to Nietzsche's arguments in the Second Essay of the

Genealogy of Morality, by applying their thinking to modern-day capitalism: "It is in credit, and not exchange, that Nietzsche sees the archetype of social organization."[18] We should emphasize once and for all that the disappearance or nonexistence of exchange does not follow from this assertion, but rather that exchange functions according to a logic not of equality but rather of a power imbalance, a power differential.

Viewing debt as the archetype of social relations means two things. On the one hand, it means conceiving economy and society on the basis of an asymmetry of power and not on that of a commercial exchange that implies and presupposes equality. It introduces power differentials between social groups and redefines money, since debt is immediately present as a command, as the power of destruction/creation over the economy and society. On the other hand, from this perspective debt means immediately making the economy subjective, since debt is an economic relation which, in order to exist, implies the molding and control of subjectivity such that "labor" becomes indistinguishable from "work on the self." Throughout the present essay we intend to corroborate, in light of debt, a truth concerning the entire history of capitalism: what one defines as "economy" would be quite simply impossible without the production and control of subjectivity and its forms of life.

The authors of *Anti-Oedipus*, in which the theory of debt is for the first time extensively developed and exploited, always stayed loyal to Marx and in particular to his theory of money. In an interview from 1988, during a period of rapid neoliberal expansion, Deleuze emphasized the importance of returning to the Marxian concept of money: "Beyond the state it is money that rules, money that communicates, and what we need these days definitely isn't any critique of Marxism, but a modern theory of money as good as Marx's that proceeds from where he left off."[19] Deleuze and Guattari interpret Marxian theory starting from the relationship between creditor and debtor and at the same time from the univocity of the concept of production. The production of subjectivity, of forms of life, of forms of existence, is not part of a superstructure, but rather of an "economic" infrastructure. Moreover, in the current economy, the production of subjectivity reveals itself to be the primary and most important form of production, the "commodity" that goes into the production of all other commodities.

With regard to money, the authors maintain that it does not derive from exchange, from mere circulation, from the commodity; nor does it constitute the sign or representation of labor. It is instead the expression of an asymmetry of forces, a power to prescribe and impose modes of future exploitation, domination, and subjection. Money is first of all debt-money, created *ex nihilo*, which has no material equivalent other than its power to destroy/create social relations and, in particular, modes of subjectivation.

This theoretical focus seems to us essential in understanding how the creditor-debtor relationship shapes all social relations in neoliberal economies. The point is not to offer a new totalizing theory of neoliberalism, but rather to prepare the groundwork for a reexamination of the current transformations affecting Western societies through the debt economy.

2

THE GENEALOGY OF DEBT
AND THE DEBTOR

DEBT AND SUBJECTIVITY: NIETZSCHE'S CONTRIBUTION

The Creditor-Debtor Relationship as the Basis of Social Relations

The debt economy appears to have produced a major change in our societies. We are going to analyze the meaning of the change by drawing on the Second Essay of the *Genealogy of Morality*.

The neoliberal economy is a subjective economy, that is, an economy that solicits and produces processes of subjectivation whose model is no longer centered, as in classical economics, on the barterer and the producer. Over the course of the 1980s and 1990s, the model was exemplified by the entrepreneur (of the self), according to the definition of Foucault, who described with the concept the mobilization, engagement, and activation of subjectivity through the techniques of business management and social government. With the series of financial crises, it is rather the "indebted man" who appears instead to embody the subjective figure of modern-day capitalism. The condition of the indebted man, which was already present, since it represents the very heart of neoliberal strategy, now occupies the totality of public space. All the designations of the social divisions of labor in neoliberal societies ("consumer," "beneficiary," "worker," "entrepreneur," "unemployed," "tourist," etc.) are now invested by the subjective figure of the "indebted man," which transforms them into indebted consumers, indebted welfare users, and, finally, as in the case with Greece, indebted citizens. If it is not individual debt, it is public debt that weighs, literally, on every individual's life, since every individual must take responsibility for it.

For a long time I thought that the subjective implication resulted mainly from changes in the organization of labor. I would like to qualify that position with a complementary hypothesis. It is debt and the creditor-debtor relationship that make up the subjective paradigm of modern-day capitalism, in which "labor" is coupled with "work on the self," in which economic activity and the ethico-political activity of producing the subject go hand in hand. Debt breeds, subdues, manufactures, adapts, and shapes subjectivity. What kind of subjectivity? With what kind of machinery does debt produce the subject?

Nietzsche covered the essential points. In the Second Essay of *On the Genealogy of Morality*, he sweeps aside in one stroke the whole of the social sciences. The constitution of society and the domestication of man ("to breed a tame and civilized animal, a *household pet*, out of the beast of prey 'man'"[1]) result neither from economic exchange (contrary to the thesis advanced by the entire tradition of political economics, from the Physiocrats to Marx by way of Adam Smith), nor from symbolic exchange (contrary to the anthropological and psychoanalytic theoretical traditions), but from the relation between creditor and debtor. Nietzsche thus makes credit the paradigm of social relations by rejecting any explanation "à l'anglaise," that is, any explanation based on exchange or interest.

What is credit/debt in its most elementary sense? A promise of payment. What is a financial asset, a share, or bond? The promise of future value. "Promise," "value," and "future" are also key words in Nietzsche's Second Essay. For Nietzsche, the "oldest and most personal relationship there is" is that between creditor and debtor, a relationship wherein "person met person for the first time, and *measured himself* person against person."[2] Consequently, the task of a community or society has first of all been to engender a person capable of *promising*, someone able to *stand guarantor for himself* in the creditor-debtor relationship, that is, capable of honoring his debt. Making a person capable of keeping a promise means constructing a memory for him, endowing him with interiority, a conscience, which provide a bulwark against forgetting. It is within the domain of debt obligations that memory, subjectivity, and conscience begin to be produced.

In commenting on these passages from the *Genealogy*, Deleuze and Guattari point out that man is created through the repression of biocosmic memory and through the constitution of a memory of the words (one's word) through which the promise is made.[3] But even if the promise implies a memory of speech and will, it is not enough to utter the promise to be clear of the debt. The Second Essay offers an excellent demystification of how the "performative" functions. The performative utterance of the promise, if it is to perform rather than describe the act of promising, is not in itself the repayment of the debt. The promise is no doubt a "speech act," but humanity produces a multiplicity of techniques, all "scarier and more sinister" from one to the next, in order to ensure that the performative does not remain mere speech, a *flatus vocis*. The performative of the promise implies and presupposes a "mnemotechnics" of cruelty and a mnemotechnics of pain, which, like the machine of Kafka's penal colony, inscribe the promise of debt repayment on the body itself. "A thing must be burnt in so that it stays in the memory: only something that continues to *hurt* stays in the memory."[4]

In the same way, "confidence," "trust," those magic words of every financial crisis, repeated like an incantation by every flunky of the debt economy (journalists, economists, politicians, experts), are not guaranteed solely through enunciation; they also require tangible and intangible collateral.

> The debtor, in order to inspire confidence that the promise of repayment will be honored, in order to give a guarantee of the solemnity and sanctity of his promise, and in order to etch the duty and obligation of repayment into his conscience, pawns something to the creditor by means of the contract in case he does not pay, something that he still "possesses" and controls, for example, his body, or his wife, or his freedom, or his life (or, in certain religious circumstances, even his after-life, the salvation of his soul, finally, even his peace in the grave…).[5]

The sphere of debt obligations thus represents the origin of those "dismal things" (Nietzsche), the moral concepts "blame," "guilt," "conscience," "bad conscience," "repression," "duty," "sacred duty," etc. In addition, breeding an animal to promise assumes that another task has already been accomplished: that of "*making* man to a certain degree necessary, uniform, a peer amongst peers, orderly and consequently predictable."[6] Through the morality of custom, "the actual labor of man on himself," and "the social straitjacket, man was *made* truly predictable."[7]

Debt therefore implies subjectivation, what Nietzsche calls the "labor of man on himself," a "self-torture." This labor produces the individual subject, a subject answerable and indebted to his creditor. Debt as economic relation, for it to take effect, has thus the peculiarity of demanding ethico-political labor constitutive of the subject. Modern-day capitalism seems to have discovered on its own the technique described by Nietzsche of constructing a person capable of promising: labor goes hand in hand with work on the self, with self-torture, with self-directed action. Debt involves a process of subjectivation that marks at once "body" and "spirit." We should note, too, that Foucault, Deleuze, and Guattari all advance a *non-economistic* concept of the economy (economic production involves the production and control of subjectivity and forms of life; economy presupposes a "morality of custom"; desire is part of the "infrastructure") based on their reading of Nietzsche.

Man is a "calculating animal." But the origin of calculation, measure, evaluation, comparison, and accounting (all of which are also functions of money) must not be sought in economic exchange or in labor but in debt. Indeed, equivalence and measure are not the products of exchange, but of the calculation of guarantees of debt repayment:

> [T]he creditor could inflict all kinds of dishonor and torture on the body of the debtor, for example, cutting as much flesh off as seemed appropriate for the debt: from this standpoint there were everywhere, early on, estimates which went into horrifyingly minute and fastidious detail, *legally* drawn up estimates for individual limbs and parts of the body.[8]

Here once again, the economy seems to have become Nietzschean. Its measures are no longer solely objective (labor time) but also subjective because founded on mechanisms of evaluation—hence the economic power of public opinion in our societies.

The concept of debt also affects the sociopolitical paradigms of our apprehension and the genealogy of social relations and institutions. The asymmetry of power constitutive of debt rids us of the "dream" according to which the State and society begin with a contract (or, in the updated version, a convention): "Whoever can command, whoever is a 'master' by nature […] what is he going to care about contracts!"[9] It also precludes our imagining the process through which society is constituted as a passage from the state of nature to society and politics. The processes constitutive of society do not involve progressive changes, consent, agreement, or delegation, but "ruptures," "leaps," and "constraints." It is only through the latter that new contracts and agreements are established.

If more proof of this state of affairs were needed, one need only look at how neoliberalism has imposed itself. Surely not by contract or agreement, but by theft, violence, and usurpation. The original accumulation of capital is always contemporaneous with its expansion; accumulation is not an historical stage, but an ever-renewed actuality.

The Temporality of Debt as Possibility, Choice, and Decision

A society dominated by banking activity, and therefore by credit, uses *time and expectation,* uses *the future, as if all these activities were overwhelmingly calculated in advance, ahead of society itself, through anticipation and deduction.*

— Jean-Joseph Goux, "Cash, check or charge?"

The most important issue raised in the Second Essay of the *Genealogy* is temporality and the "ethico-political" subjectivation that follows from it, for the memory that must be created is not one for conserving the past, but a memory of the future. No less for the creditor than the debtor, "a memory straining toward the future" must be made for man "so that he [...] is answerable for his own *future*!"[10]

What is credit? A promise to pay a debt, a promise to repay in a more or less distant and unpredictable future, since it is subject to the radical uncertainty of time. For Nietzsche, making a memory for man means being able "to have [...] control over the future," "to view the future as the present and anticipate it," so that he is answerable for his own future.[11] Granting credit requires one to estimate that which is inestimable—future behavior and events—and to expose oneself to the uncertainty of time. The system of debt must therefore neutralize time, that is, the risk inherent to it. It must anticipate and ward off every potential "deviation" in the behavior of the debtor the future might hold.

In the light of the neoliberal debt economy, the Second Essay of the *Genealogy* takes on a new topicality: debt is not only an economic mechanism, it is also a security-state technique of government aimed at reducing the uncertainty of the behavior of the governed. By training the governed to "promise" (to honor their debt), capitalism exercises "control over the future," since debt obligations allow one to foresee, calculate, measure, and establish equivalences between current and future behavior. The effects of the power of debt on subjectivity (guilt and responsibility) allow capitalism to bridge the gap between present and future.

The debt economy is an economy of time and subjectivation in a specific sense. Indeed, neo-liberalism is an economy turned toward the future, since finance is a promise of future wealth and, consequently, incommensurable with actual wealth. No use making a fuss because the economy's "present" and "future" fail to match up! What matters is finance's goal of reducing what will be to what is, that is, reducing the future and its possibilities to current power relations. From this perspective, all financial innovations have but one sole purpose: possessing the future in advance by objectivizing it. This objectivation is of a completely different order from that of labor time; objectivizing time, possessing it in advance, means subordinating all possibility of choice and decision which the future holds to the reproduction of capitalist power relations. In this way, debt appropriates not only the present labor time of wage-earners and of the population in general, it also preempts non-chronological time, each person's future as well as the future of society as a whole. The principal explanation for the strange sensation of living in a society without time, without possibility, without foreseeable rupture, is debt.

The relationship between time and debt, money lending and the lender's appropriation of time, has been well-known for centuries. If in the Middle Ages the distinction between usury and interest was not well-established—the former being considered but an excess of the latter (ah! the wisdom of our forebears!)—one did, however, have a very specific idea of what the money lender "stole" and the nature of his fault: he sold time, that which did not belong to him and whose sole owner was God. "What indeed does he sell, if not the time that elapses between the moment he lends the money and the moment he is repaid, with interest? Time, of course, belongs solely to God. As a thief of time, the usurer steals God's patrimony."[12]

For Marx, the historical importance of the usurious loan (a "primitive name for interest") lies in the fact that, unlike consumer wealth, the usurious loan represents a generative process comparable to (and a precursor of) that of capital, that is, of money that generates money. A manuscript from the 13th century cited by Jacques Le Goff does a fine job of summarizing the latter point and the sort of time the money lender appropriates—not only labor time but living time:

Usurers sin against nature by wanting to make money give birth to money, as a horse gives birth to a horse, or a mule to a mule. Usurers are in addition thieves [*latrines*], for they sell time that does not belong to them, and selling someone else's property, despite its owner, is theft. In addition, since they sell nothing other than the expectation of money, that is to say, time, they sell days and nights. But the day is the time of clarity, and the night is the time for repose. Consequently, they sell light and repose. It is, therefore, not just for them to receive eternal light and eternal rest.[13]

Whereas in the Middle Ages time belonged to God and God alone, today, as possibility, creation, choice, and decision, it is the primary object of capitalist expropriation/appropriation. If we distance ourselves from the economic point of view in which everyone seems to be caught up, what are the enormous quantities of money concentrated in banks, insurance, pension funds, etc., and manipulated by finance but potentialities, immense concentrations of possibilities? Finance sees to it that the only choices and the only possible decisions are those of the tautology of money making money, of production for the sake of production. Whereas in industrial societies there still existed an "open" time—in the form of progress or revolution—today, the future and its possibilities, quashed by the huge sums of money mobilized by finance and devoted to reproducing capitalist power relations, seem to be frozen. For debt simply neutralizes time, time as the creation of new possibilities, that is to say, the raw material of all political, social, or esthetic change. Debt harnesses and exercises the power of destruction/creation, the power of choice and decision.

The Economy as Process of Subjectivation

In addition to establishing the creditor-debtor relation as social paradigm, Nietzsche's Second Essay holds another fundamental lesson that must be expanded upon. As we have said, the creditor-debtor relationship is inextricably an economy and an "ethics," since it presupposes, in order for the debtor to stand as "self"-guarantor, an ethico-political process of constructing a subjectivity endowed with a memory, a conscience, and a morality that forces him to be both accountable and guilty. Economic production and the production of subjectivity, labor and ethics, are indissociable.

The debt economy thus intensifies what traditional political economics had already discovered, namely, that the essence of wealth is subjective. Here "subjective" not only means making available physical and intellectual capacities and time (labor time) in exchange for wages, but also the production of individual subjectivity. In this sense, the debt economy changes the concepts of both "labor" and "politics." It seems to me that my friends in cognitive capitalism are mistaken when they make "knowledge" the origin of valorization and exploitation. There is nothing new in the fact that science, skills, and technological and organizational innovations represent *the* productive forces of capital—Marx already understood as much in the mid-19th century. But the so-called knowledge economy fails to account for most of the class relations the theory of cognitive capitalism attributes to it. It is but one mechanism, one type of activity, one site of power relations alongside multiple other activities and power relations. Indeed, it must submit to the imperatives of the debt economy (savage cuts in "cognitive" investments, in culture, education, public services, etc.). In any case, knowledge cannot provide the basis for the class struggle for either capital or the "governed."

What is required, and cuts across the economy and modern-day society, is not knowledge but the injunction to become an economic "subject" ("human capital," "entrepreneur of the self"), an injunction that concerns just as much the unemployed as the user of public services, the consumer, the most "modest" of workers, the poorest, or the "migrant." In the debt economy, to become human capital or an entrepreneur of the self means assuming the costs as well as the risks of a flexible and financialized economy, costs and risks which are not only—far from it—those of innovation, but also and especially those of precariousness, poverty, unemployment, a failing health system, housing shortages, etc. To make an enterprise of oneself (Foucault)—that means taking responsibility for poverty, unemployment, precariousness, welfare benefits, low wages, reduced pensions, etc., as if these were the individual's "resources" and "investments" to manage as capital, as "his" capital. As we can very clearly see, the concepts of entrepreneur of the self and human capital must be interpreted by way of the creditor-debtor relationship. We must start from the most general and most deterritorialized power relation through which neoliberal power governs the class struggle.

In the current crisis, the "most" that capitalism demands and compels, in every area, is less knowledge than that one *take upon oneself* the costs and risks externalized by the State and corporations. Differentials in productivity do not first derive from "knowledge" or information, but from the subjective undertaking of these costs and risks, whether in the production of knowledge, the activities of the user, or whatever other kind of activity. It is this "subjectivation," in addition to "labor" in the classical sense of the term, that—to speak like the economists of capital—makes productivity grow. The subjective figure of this undertaking is that of the debtor affected by guilt, bad conscience, and responsibility. As the crisis has worsened, his entrepreneurial contours have faded and the epic panegyrics to the glory of innovation and knowledge that accompanied the beginnings of neoliberalism have fallen silent.

If capitalists spend little time worrying about investing in a more than improbable—always heralded but never realized—"knowledge society," they are, on the other hand, cruelly inflexible when forcing the governed to take on all the economic risks and damage the capitalists themselves have created. In the sovereign debt crisis, there is no question of knowledge, cognitive capitalism, creativity, and cultural capitalism. And yet it is on these grounds that capital has chosen to wage its class struggle. The debt economy, then, is characterized by a twofold expansion of the exploitation of subjectivity: extensive (since not only are industrial work and tertiary sector concerned but every activity and condition) and intensive (since it encompasses the relationship to the self, in the guise of the entrepreneur of the self—who is at once responsible for "his" capital and guilty of poor management—whose paradigm is the "unemployed").

The debt economy also occupies the terrain of the political, since it uses and exploits the process of "ethico-political" constitution in order to transform each individual into an indebted economic subject. These transformations of capitalism that affect life and subjectivity do not in the least seem to have entered into the political theories of Rancière and Badiou. Why bother with the debt economy, with the exploitation of "work on the self" and the appropriation/expropriation of time as opportunity, choice, and decision, when the process of political subjectivation always plays out in the same way starting from the universal question of equality—whether in the Greek polis or in the Roman empire (the slave revolt), the French Revolution, the Paris Commune, or the Russian Revolution? It would be a waste of time to bother with these transformations since the revolution cannot arise from "economics." For Rancière and Badiou, politics is independent of "economics" solely because the image they have of it and of capitalism in general is the one—a caricature—served up by economists themselves. Contrary to these revolutionary, democratic, or simply economic theories, the force of capitalism lies in its ability to link "economics" (and communication, consumption, the Welfare State, etc.) and the production of subjectivity in different ways. To say with Badiou and Rancière that political subjectivation cannot be understood to follow from economics is obviously completely different from asking what their paradoxical articulation is. The former perspective exemplifies the illusion of a "pure" politics, since subjectivation, attached to nothing at all, can never establish the ground necessary for it to exist. On the other hand, the latter perspective opens a space for political construction and experimentation, since subjectivation must, if it is to exist, create a rupture by *retraversing* and *reconfiguring* the economic, the social, the political, and so on.

A Very Nietzschean Marx

An essay from Marx's youth, "Comments on James Mill," allows us to flesh out the nature of the creditor-debtor relationship.[14] In the text, which is extraordinary for a number of reasons, Marx delineates a credit relation quite different form that analyzed in the third volume of *Capital*. In the latter, which is in fact a collection of more or less finished notes, credit is only one of the three forms of capital (financial, industrial, and commercial) and the creditor/debtor relationship is dealt with as simply an affair among capitalists. Conversely, in

"Comments on James Mill," the "poor man" is the debtor and the creditor passes "moral" judgment on him in evaluating his solvency. The poor man's "social virtues," the "content of his vital activity," his "flesh and blood," his "morality," and even his "existence" are measured as guarantees of repayment. These pages from Marx's youth help to fill out our understanding of the "indebted man" as the conceptual figure we have begun to delineate with Nietzsche's precious help.

For Marx, the creditor-debtor relation is at once different from and complementary to the labor-capital relation. If we put aside the content of the relation between creditor and debtor (money), we see that credit does not solicit and exploit *labor* but rather *ethical action* and the *work of self-constitution at both an individual and collective level.* The credit relation does not mobilize physical and intellectual abilities as labor does (material or immaterial, it makes no difference), but the morality of the debtor, his mode of existence (his "ethos"). The importance of the debt economy lies in the fact that it appropriates and exploits both chronological labor time and *action*, non-chronological time, time as choice, decision, a wager on what will happen and on the forces (trust, desire, courage, etc.) that make choice, decision, and action possible. As Marx put it in 1844:

> In the credit system, of which banking is the perfect expression, it appears as if the power of the alien, material force were broken, the relationship of self-estrangement abolished and man had once more human relations to man.

Credit *appears* to run counter to the market and the capital-labor relation. It makes it seem that social relations between people are no longer inversed in a social relationship between things, as is the case in the capital/labor relationship. Commodity fetishism ("the alien, material force") no longer seems operative since man is directly confronted with his fellow man by giving him his "trust."

> But this abolition of estrangement, this return of man to himself and therefore to other men is only an appearance; the self-estrangement, the dehumanization, is all the more infamous and extreme because its element is no longer commodity, metal, paper, but man's *moral existence*, man's *social existence*, *the inmost depths of his heart*, and because under the appearance of man's *trust* in man it is the height of *distrust* and complete estrangement. (My emphasis.)

Still more than labor, credit attains and manifests the subjective essence of production, since what is at stake, according to another translation of the same passage, is "the moral existence, the communal existence, the innermost depths of the human heart." In order to act, that is, in order to begin something whose accomplishment is subject to the vicissitudes of time, to take a chance on the unknown, the unforeseeable, the uncertain, other forces are needed than those engaged in labor: trust in others, in oneself, and in the world. The creditor-debtor relation represents only the "illusion" of the end of man's subordination to the production of economic "value," the illusion of his rise to a "production of values" no longer founded on wage labor, the market, and the commodity, but on the community and the noblest sentiments of the human heart (trust, desire, man's recognition by his fellow man, etc.). With credit, Marx tells us, alienation is complete, since it is the ethical work constitutive of the self and the community that is exploited.

Trust, the condition for action, becomes universal distrust, turning into a demand for "security." The circulation of private debt is a circulation of selfish and individual interests. It presupposes, in the guise of another person's recognition, a preliminary distrust, since the other person is a rival, a competitor and/or a debtor.

What constitutes the essence of credit? We leave entirely out of account here the content of credit, which is again money. We leave out of account, therefore, the content of this trust in accordance with which a man recognizes another man by advancing him a certain quantity of value and— at best, namely, when he does not demand payment for the credit, i.e., he is not a usurer— showing his trust in his fellow man not being a swindler, but a "good" man. By a "good" man, the one who bestows his trust understands, like Shylock, a man who is "able to pay."

The trust that credit exploits has nothing to do with the belief in new possibilities in life and, thus, in some noble sentiment toward oneself, others, and the world. It is limited to a trust in solvency and makes solvency the content and measure of the ethical relationship. The "moral" concepts of good and bad, of trust and distrust, here translate into solvency and insolvency. The "moral" categories by which we take the "measure" of man and his actions are a measure of (the) economic reason (of debt). In capitalism, then, solvency serves as the measure of the "morality" of man.

And even in the case where "a rich man gives credit to a poor man," which constituted an exception and not the rule at the time, Marx remarks that

the life of the poor man and his talents and activity serve the rich man as a guarantee of the repayment of the money lent. That means, therefore, that all the *social* virtues of the poor man, the content of his *vital* activity, his *existence* itself, represent for the rich man the reimbursement of his capital with the customary interest. Hence the death of the poor man is the worst eventuality for the creditor. It is the death of his capital together with the interest. (My emphasis.)

Credit entails the creditor's "moral judgment" of the debtor, that is, a "subjective" measure of value. But not only are the skills and know-how of the worker evaluated, so too are the poor man's actions in society (social "virtues," "conduct," "reputation"), that is, his lifestyle, his social behavior, his values, his very *existence*. It is through debt that capital is able to appropriate not only the physical and intellectual abilities the poor man employs in his labor, but also his social and existential forces.

One ought to consider how vile it is to estimate the value of a man in money, as happens in the credit relationship. [...] Credit is the economic judgment on the morality of a man. In credit, the man himself, instead of metal or paper, has become the mediator of exchange, not however as a man, but as the mode of existence of capital and interest. The medium of exchange, therefore, has certainly returned out of its material form and been put back in man, but only because the man himself has been put outside himself...

Credit, then, not only exploits social relationships in general, but also the uniqueness of existence. It exploits the process of subjectivation by affecting the individuation of existence itself. After all, the "moral" judgment has to do with "life." And yet the "life" in question is not biological life (health, birth, and death), as with the concept of biopolitics, and still less cognitive life, but "existential" life. Existence here means the power of self-affirmation, the force of self-positioning, the choices that found and bear with them modes and styles of life. The content of money here is not labor but existence, individuality, and human morality; the material of money is not labor time, but the time of existence:

> Within the credit relationship, it is not the case that money is transcended in man, but that man himself is turned into money, or money is incorporated in him. Human individuality, human morality itself, has become both an object of commerce and the material in which money exists. Instead of money, or paper, it is my own personal existence, my flesh and blood, my social virtue and importance, which constitutes the material, corporeal form of the spirit of money. Credit no longer resolves the value of money into money but into human flesh and the human heart.

Marx's text intersects with Nietzsche's on several points. The credit relation mobilizes and exploits the "morality of custom," the ethico-political constitution of the self and the community. Its operations are inscribed in the body engaged in producing "social virtue." But unlike Nietzsche, Marx is not concerned with "primitive" societies, but with the capitalist economy to which domesticated man is bound.

"Objective" Debt in Marx's *Capital*

A second reading from Marx. It is helpful to return briefly to the theory of credit Marx advances in the third volume of *Capital*. We do so in order to better understand the changing place credit has in Marx's work. If in the first text we looked at Marx deals with what we can call subjective or existential debt, here he deals with *objective* debt. He does not go back to the rich analyses of debt's subjective effects developed in his youth. By focusing solely on its "systemic" functions, he nonetheless disposes of certain received ideas which observers of the financial crisis never fail to repeat.

First of all, the speculative, parasitic, usurious character of financial capital is inseparable from its functional role: "A bank represents on the one hand the centralization of money capital, of the lenders, and on the other hand the centralization of the borrowers."[15] Second, although it takes different forms (commercial, industrial, monetary, financial), there is only one capital and one valorization process. Already in Marx's day it was absurd to separate a "real economy" from a supposedly "financial economy." The formula for financial capital, that is, self-valorizing money (M-M'), fully captures the logic of capital. For Westerners, for the most part Christian, it should not be difficult to follow Marx's reasoning: value appears as a "self-moving substance," of which industrial, commercial, and financial capital are but particular forms. As in theology, where the Holy Trinity encompasses the Father, Son, and Holy Spirit, capital encompasses three different forms—industrial, commercial, and financial.

But Marx goes much further still. Calling capitalists every name in the book ("honorable bandits," "usurers"—even though for him there are no good capitalists, industrialists, and bad capitalists, financiers, or bankers), Marx has the clear-sightedness all the observers lack, especially those on the left. Already in his day Marx defined the specific place held by financial capital with respect to industrial capital: on the one hand, the former represents the "common" capital of the class; on the other hand, money concentrated in banks is "potential" money, unlike industrial capital which is actual money. Money in banks represents future wealth, that is, the possibility of choices and decisions over future production and power relations. In its financial form, capital accumulated in banks appears as "capital in general," a simple abstraction. But it is a powerful abstraction, since capital emerges as "autonomous value," "independent" of its actualization in a particular sphere; it exists as an "undifferentiated" force capable of every form of actualization. It thus appears as the power to prescribe and anticipate future value, as a power of destruction/creation.

On the money market it is only lenders and borrowers who face one another. The commodity has the same form, money. All particular forms of capital, arising from its investment in particular spheres of production or circulation, are obliterated here. It exists in the undifferentiated, self-identical form of independent value, of money. Competition between particular spheres now ceases; they are all thrown together as borrowers of money, and capital confronts them all in a form still indifferent to the specific manner and mode of its application.[16]

Because it is undifferentiated, capital thus appears as the common capital of the capitalist class only in the financial sphere: "Here capital really does emerge, in the pressure of its demand and supply, as *the common capital of the class*, whereas industrial capital appears like this only in the movement and competition between the particular spheres."[17] Capitalist organization becomes subjective not by way of the industrial capitalist (who is now no more than a function of the management of production), but by way of the financial capitalist (an owner whose possibility of making decisions and choices has been deterritorialized). Unlike various forms of industrial capital, financial capital is made to represent the interests of "social capital."

> On top of this, with the development of large-scale industry money capital emerges more and more, in so far as it appears on the market, as not represented by the individual capitalist, the proprietor of this or that fraction of the mass of capital on the market, but rather as a concentrated and organized mass, placed under the control of the bankers as representatives of the social capital in a quite different manner to real production.[18]

It is its general form, its indifference to any kind of industrial specificity, that is, as it emerges through credit, that allows capital to exploit the social sphere.

> [C]redit offers the individual capitalist [...] an absolute command over the capital and property

of others, within certain limits, and, through this, command over other people's labor. It is disposal over social capital, rather than his own, that gives him command over social labor.[19]

For Lenin, who returns to and develops Marx's point of view at a time that in many ways resembles our own, banks and bankers play a political role of the utmost importance, since they provide "coherence" and strategies to industrial capitalists whose interests are too diverse to represent the capitalist class: "The concentration of capital and the growth of their turnover is radically changing the significance of the banks. Scattered capitalists are transformed into a single collective."[20] The "coherence" and strategies are those of the M-M' logic, which by making money from money also reveals its "irrationality." The latter materializes in every "liberal" period and leads almost automatically to the most severe crises, each time clearing the way for authoritarian politics (which happened with the First World War and fascism).

Action and Confidence within the Logic of Debt

With the debt economy, it is no longer possible to distinguish *labor* from *action*, as Hannah Arendt was still able to do. With credit, action becomes part of the economic dynamics, and even its driving force. Through the subjectivation involved in debt, modern-day capitalism encompasses action as well as the forces that make it possible. Indeed, debt exploits *the ethical action constitutive of the individual and the community* by mobilizing forces that are at the basis of "man's moral existence, man's social existence." Among these forces, we are going to focus in particular on "confidence," that magic word of the current crisis which, beyond its contagious use among economists, journalists, and experts, is one of the symptoms of the shifting frontiers of capitalist exploitation.

To reconstruct the concepts of action and confidence, we will have to indulge in a short philosophical digression which the reader may possibly wish to skip. It will allow us to better appreciate how and why capitalism sets its sights on action, that is, non-chronological time, and thus on the ability to choose and decide what is good and what is bad.

According to the theory of action of the American pragmatist William James, every time we are confronted with a veritable choice, an important existential alternative, because it fulfills certain possibilities and eliminates others, as in the case with "moral" problems, the choice does not solely depend—far from it—on the understanding, on "cognition," or knowledge.[21] The alternative first calls on our "active propensities," our "most intimate powers," our "passional natures," our "most cherished powers" that is, the "innermost depths of the human heart" which Marx speaks of and which James defines as a set of active forces ("fortitude, hope, rapture, admiration, earnestness, and the like"), bringing them together within the concept of "desire."[22]

Measure, assessment, and evaluation "of what is good, or would be good if it did exist" do not originate in philosophical speculation or in scientific knowledge. "Science can tell us what exists; but to compare *worths*, both of what exists and of what does not exist, we must consult not science, but what Pascal calls our heart." Our power to act and its "success [depend] on energy to act; energy again depends on faith that we shall not fail."[23] It depends, that is, on the faith/confidence in what we do, on the faith/confidence in the world and others. Action depends, finally, on the intensity of faith/confidence and the latter on "active propensities," on emotions, and on the most intimate powers of the human heart. James defines faith/confidence as a "willingness to act." Apprehension of the power to act springs from "subjective method, the method of belief based on desire."[24]

But the faith/confidence or willingness to act can be described in two different ways. In one instance, it is faith-habit, and in the other, faith-confidence that induces action. In the first, the world is determined, accomplished, everything is already given, in such a way that faith is the faith in already-established beliefs. In the second, which is what interests us here, the world is still coming into existence. It is incomplete, undetermined, and this incompleteness and indetermination call on our power to act and the latter on faith. This second conception of confidence is mobilized and redirected by credit (capitalism's force is not only negative; it lies in its ability to redirect passions, desires, and action to its own advantage), for credit anticipates a future action whose result cannot be guaranteed in advance. Credit is a mechanism of power that bears on undetermined possibilities and whose actualization/realization is subject to a radical and not probabilistic uncertainty.

Our uncertain, unstable, and changing world is, to use Walter Benjamin's words, a world "poor" in experience since, as James reminds us, experience is always changing. But it is precisely the poverty of experience (we do not know what tomorrow holds) that summons up the confidence (faith), desire, the innermost depths of the human heart, necessary to take a chance on this uncertain world. These forces are excited and intensified by the indetermination of the future. Indeed, what does the poverty of experience demand of us? "To start from scratch; to make a new start," Benjamin writes. The "barbarian," which for Benjamin describes contemporary man, "sees nothing permanent. But for this very reason he sees ways everywhere […]. Because he sees ways everywhere, he always stands at a crossroads. No moment can know what the next will bring."[25] Confidence transforms the poverty of experience into a politics of "experimentation."[26]

How do we act in this world, how do we venture an action whose outcome is uncertain, if we cannot know what the future holds? In order to act under these conditions, confidence ("faith") in oneself is necessary, confidence in the world and in others. A tacit agreement with oneself, the world, and others must be made in order to act in a world where "routine maxims" are incapable of guiding action. Action thus represents a leap into the unknown which "knowledge" has no way of helping us to make. Our skepticism and our political impasses are not cognitive but ethical, since "we live forward but think backward," as James puts it. To live forward means "to believe in the world and in the new possibilities of life" it encompasses, says Deleuze. Faith and trust are a force—joyous and confident—that gives one a "generous strength."

Confidence, trust, is thus the condition of all acts of creation, whether artistic, ethical, or political. According to James, modern man must be comfortable with this "barbaric" world, since his power to act is not brought to bear on raw facts but on possibilities, which, according to Guattari's definition, are a "matter of choice, a matter of options" (one must choose because the possibilities are "ambiguous," virtualities holding different alternatives). The fact that we are in the world with our perceptions, sensations, and knowledge is still not enough to act. In order for the power to act to become effective, possibility must exceed actuality. The world must contain indetermination, an open temporality in the process of realizing itself, that is, a "present" which encompasses possible alternatives and, thus, possibilities of choice and existential risks. It is these possibilities and these unpredictable alternatives that debt seeks to neutralize.

The "barbarians," the pluralists, "demand in [the universe] a *character* for which our emotions and active propensies shall be a match." Desire and trust act on a "moving present," that is, a "zone of formative processes" which is the "zone of the individual differences, and of the social 'twists' which by common confession they initiate." This zone is "the dynamic belt of quivering uncertainty, the line where past and future meet."[27] In order to realize the power to act, we need to believe (trust) in the "moving present," the present as possibility, that is, in the world and the new possibilities of life that it holds. The power to act is subordinate to an existential affirmation, to a "yes" that expresses a self-positioning. It presupposes hope and faith, anticipating what has not yet come to pass, making the impossible possible.

In the "barbarian" world, trust and hope (passions, emotions, desire) depend less on taking a stand, making a commitment, relative to existing beliefs, than on a self-validation of new beliefs, new values, new connections, new meanings, and new forms of life. Conversely, fear, sad affects and passions serve to neutralize the power to act.[28] Finance is a formidable instrument for controlling the temporality of action, neutralizing possibilities, the "moving present," "quivering uncertainty," and "the line where past and future meet." It locks up possibilities within an established framework while at the same time projecting them into the future. For finance, the future is a mere forecast of current domination and exploitation. But if a critical threshold of uncertainty with regard to future of exploitation and domination is passed, the present, emptied of its possibilities, collapses. The crisis is then a crisis of time from which emerges a time of political and social creation, which finance can only endeavor to destroy. This is exactly our present situation. The logic of debt is stifling our possibilities for action.

We now turn our attention to Deleuze and Guattari's examination of debt in its historical development in order to better appreciate the specificity of the logic of debt in the modern-day economy. Debt resurfaces in the late 1960s and early 1970s in the work of Deleuze and Guattari as a way of analyzing contemporary capitalism. By bringing together Nietzsche's theory of credit in primitive societies and Marx's theory of money in capitalism, the authors trace a short history of debt that encourages a non-economistic reading of the economy, a reading not based on exchange but rather on an asymmetrical creditor-debtor power relation. A non-economistic interpretation of the economy means, on the one hand, that economic production is inseparable from the production and control of subjectivity and its forms of existence, on the other hand, that money, before fulfilling the economic functions of measure, means of exchange, payment, and accumulation, manifests the power to command and distribute the places and tasks assigned to the governed.

In his courses at the University of Vincennes from 1971 to 1973, Deleuze returns to considerations developed with Guattari in *Anti-Oedipus* regarding the Marxian theory of money.[29] By reexamining it from the perspective of the asymmetry of the credit relation, that is, the asymmetry inherent in the economy of debt, they establish the basis for an understanding of money in which economic and political functions are indistinguishable. They thus draw on the concept of "power" advanced by Foucault in his own rereading of Nietzsche in order to better elucidate money. Capital is above all a power to command and prescribe exercised through the power of destruction/creation of money.

Anti-Oedipus and the university courses, conceived and written well before the institution of neoliberal policies, help us to understand why debt and finance, far from being pathologies of capitalism, far from expressions of certain people's greed, constitute strategic mechanisms orienting investments and, thereby, determining the forms of "destruction" of the old and the "creation" of a new world capitalist order. The financial and banking systems are at the center of a politics of destruction/creation in which economics and politics have become inextricable. If we want to understand how powers are reconfigured by the debt economy, we must first of all establish the links between economics and politics.

In Deleuze's courses, his critique focuses on the power differentials money manifests, differentials economists have had a hard time perceiving. Capitalism objectively conceals the fact that money functions in two fundamentally different ways, as *revenue* and as *capital*. In the first case, money is a means of payment (wages and revenue). It buys a quantity of already-existing goods imposed by capitalist production. It is limited to reproducing the established power relations and forms of subjection necessary for that production. In the second, money functions as a financing structure (credit money and the quasi-money of finance). In other words, it has the possibility of choosing and deciding on future production and commodities and, therefore, on the relations of power and subjection underlying them. Money as capital preempts the future.

Money-revenue simply reproduces power relations, the division of labor, and the established functions and roles. Money as capital, on the other hand, has the ability to reconfigure those relations. Neoliberalism offers a glaring example of this. Debt-money was the strategic weapon used to destroy Fordism and create the structures of a new world capitalist order.[30] Henceforth, debt/finance is no longer a simple convention, nor a mere function of the real economy. It represents social capital and the "collective capitalist," the "common" capital of the capitalist class, as Marx and Lenin well knew.

Deleuze's position develops Marx's theory by ridding it of numerous pitfalls. He underscores the impossibility of considering a market economy in itself, since the latter derives from and is always subordinate to the money economy and to the debt economy which distribute power, subjection, and domination; the impossibility of having money originate in the commodity, but also in labor, since money, by right and in fact, precedes labor, commodities, and exchange. Money organizes them, controls them, and determines how they are distributed. The asymmetry of power, the differentials of power expressed in debt-money, hold for every society—primitive society, ancient society, feudal society, and capitalism. A circuit of exchange never structures or forms a society, a completely different kind of circuit does, one that has nothing to do with arithmetic. Equal or unequal quantities do not enter into an exchange relation, quantities of different power do, "quantities of power, in the mathematical sense of the word 'power,' different potentialities."[31]

Exchange never comes first. Indeed, no economy functions based on economic exchange; no society functions based on symbolic exchange. The economy and society are organized according to power differentials, an imbalance of potentialities. We should again emphasize that this does not mean that exchange does not exist, but rather that it functions according to a logic not of equality but of disequilibrium and difference. In primitive societies, there are no forms of exchange, there are no forms of equivalence [...], there is a system of debt and debt is fundamentally affected by a functional imbalance [...]. For example, the imbalance between giving and receiving consumer objects does not, functionally, balance out; the inequality is fundamental and constant. The thing only works imbalanced.[32]

This is precisely the argument between Leach and Lévi-Strauss, in which Leach held that inequality is a fundamental part of the system, a part of its functioning, whereas for Lévi-Strauss it is a pathological consequence of the system.

Leach is right. With each flow, with each flow entering a composite product, there is a fundamental imbalance with regard to the flows involved. The imbalance is continually compensated through a withdrawal from another flow, from a flow qualified differently. For example, the imbalance between the person who allocates consumer objects and the person who receives them will be offset by an entirely different flow, the flow of prestige whereby the person who allocates receives prestige [...]. I would even say that the economic unity in so-called primitive societies is, fundamentally, these finite combinations which—through them and through their imbalanced functioning—bring all these differently qualified flows into existence.

There is a whole circuit of debt that emerges from the circulation of its finite elements. This is the system of finite debt, and the system of alliances structures precisely this circuit of finite debt.[33]

Infinite Debt

The transition from "finite debt" to "infinite debt" with the end of primitive societies represents an event whose consequences continue to this day, since capitalism has extended the transition in order to produce the indebted man, who will never finish paying his debts. Indeed, with the arrival of the great empires—which centralized and concentrated power in "state" forms and thereby marked the end of primitive societies—and the emergence of monotheistic religions—which centralized and concentrated "spiritual" power—debt could no longer be redeemed. A system of infinite debt replaced the system of finite and mobile combinations ("I'll make you a block of alliances and kinship") of primitive societies. Christianity "stuck us with the infinite," which comes down to saying that we are in a social system in which there is no end to anything, in which indebtedness is for life.

"Debt becomes the relation of a debtor who will never finish paying to a creditor who will never finish using up the interest on the debt": "debt toward 'divinity,' toward 'society,' toward 'the State.'"[34] A stroke of Christian genius, for the "holy trinity" contains within itself the creditor and the debtor:

> God sacrificing himself for man's debt, none other than God paying himself back, God as the only one able to redeem man from what, to man himself, has become irredeemable—the creditor sacrificing himself for his debtor, out of *love* (would you credit it?—), out of love for his debtor!... [35]

Christianity, by introducing the infinite, completely reinvented the system of debt which capitalism would inherit. In imperial configurations prior to Christianity, debt was indeed infinite, since, thanks to their "state" apparatuses, and unlike in primitive societies, one could no longer reimburse, one could no longer balance the power differentials established through an ever-unequal exchange. Still, debt remained "exterior" to the individual and his conscience. The particularity of Christianity lies in the fact that it places us not only within a system of debt, but also within a system of "interiorized debt." "The pain of a debtor is interiorized, responsibility for the debt becomes a feeling of guilt."[36]

In his short history of debt, Deleuze notes another fundamental transition. Whereas the "interiorized debt" of Christianity is still transcendental, in capitalism its existence is "immanent." The infinite that Christianity introduces to religion capitalism reinvents at the economic level: the movement of capital as the self-generated movement of value, of money that makes money, and which, thanks to debt, expands beyond its limits. With capitalism, capitalist valorization and debt become infinite processes each propagating the other. Marx stresses the reproduction process by which money produces more money, through which it reveals itself as self-generating, growing on top of itself, continually overrunning its limits. Capital has immanent limits, but it reproduces them on an ever-expanding scale. The system of the infinite is the system of destruction/creation whose foremost expression can be found in and through the creation/destruction of money.

Before we address capitalism as such, let us here make a brief stop in Greece and the Middle Ages in order to corroborate the historical continuity of the debt-power-measure relation we encountered in the *Genealogy of Morality*. As Deleuze and Guattari were writing *Anti-Oedipus*, Michel Foucault developed a concept of money that, as with Deleuze and Guattari's, runs counter to the traditional interpretation that has money emerging from a market economy. "The appearance of money is linked to the constitution of a new kind of power, a power whose sole purpose is to intervene in the system of property, in the system of debts and payments."[37]

The interpretation of the market origin of money, which restricts it to the functions of representing value and utility in exchange, "by taking the sign for the thing itself, represents a kind of radical, fundamental philosophical error."[38] The institution of measure, of which money is one manifestation, does not have an "economic" origin. In Foucault's 1971 course we rediscover the measure-debt relationship established by Nietzsche, which was a major inspiration for Foucault's theory of power.

> It is easy to see how the application of measure is tied to the whole problem of peasant indebtedness, the transfer of agricultural property, the payment of credit, the equivalence between goods and manufactured items, urbanization and the establishment of state structures. At the heart of the measuring practice appears the institution of money.[39]

Economists remove trade from the complexity of power relations and make it, along with utility, the origin of society and man. A kind of "English" hypocrisy, Nietzsche might say.

Measure, evaluation, and appraisal all arise from the question of power, before there is any question of economics. The origin of valuation and measure is both religious and political: "Whether a tyrant or lawmaker, he who holds the power is the surveyor of the city: the measurer of the land, of things, wealth, rights, powers, and men."[40]

Barbarian Flows

Thanks to Deleuze's brilliant commentary of Georges Duby's *The Early Growth of European Economy*, we can enlarge upon the kind of different, inextricably economic and power flows that run through and structure the economy and society. The "economic" functions of money (measure, accumulation, general equivalency, mode of payment) depend on a flow of another kind, that is, of another power. If money is not supported by a power flow, it disappears and the economic functions of measure, the means of payment of money, disappear with it. This is what happened to the European economy after the fall of the Carolingian empire, when the flow of imperial power came to an end. The European economy was only revived through a flow of destruction/ creation, in other words, through the power of "barbarian" deterritorialization which literally resuscitated exchange and the different functions of money. The market economy had no autonomy, no possibility of existing autonomously, independent of a power flow, of a deterritorializing force.

From the far reaches of the empire the Vikings with their ships and the Hungarians with their horses (mobility, migratory, nomadic, and warrior flows whose power was greater than the peasants') descended, pillaging villages, tombs, and monasteries.

> They carried out a kind of discharge, a liberation of money throughout Europe, that injected a monetary power into the economy which money, reduced to its purchasing power or its exchange value, had completely lost. They made economic investments through destruction.[41]

The less mobile flow (the peasants) became subordinated to the nomadic and mobile flow (the barbarian warriors). The "barbarian" flows were deterritorialized as well as deterritorializing. If money as a means of payment, measure, etc., is a deterritorialized flow, its deterritorializing force did not come from money itself, but from the destructive/creative power flows set in motion by the barbarians (and later by capitalists or revolutionary forces). Powerless monetary signs received their power from the nomadic, migratory, mobile, barbarian flow. Faced with the barbarians, the peasants fled and were affected in their flight by a "secondary" deterritorializing coefficient which held a power otherwise lacking in a sedentary peasantry. The power of destruction/creation was and is not a property of money as such. Money must be transformed into capital, that is, into a power of destruction/creation. With neoliberalism, the stock market, finance, and debt are the mechanisms that effectuate this transformation.

Capitalist Flows

Deleuze insists on the point: an economy has never functioned as a market economy. Regardless of the social structure, an economy includes exchange and makes exchange networks work on the basis of money as purchasing power solely as a function of another flow. "Exchange obviously comes second relative to something of a completely different nature. [...] '[A] different nature' has a very strict sense, meaning a flow of a different power."[42]

In capitalism, the same money expresses diverse power flows. The flow of purchasing power, which represents the entirety of means of payment (wages and revenue) used in the buying of goods already produced, already present, is strictly subordinate, as a lesser power flow, to the flows of financing. The latter do not represent mere "purchasing power," a simple correspondence between money and goods, but a power for prescribing, ordering, that is, a set of possibilities for choices and decisions with regard to the future, which anticipate what the production, power relations, and forms of subjection will be. The power of money as financing structure does not derive from greater purchasing power, the capitalist's force does not depend on his being wealthier than a worker. His "power derives from the fact that he controls and determines the direction of financing flows," in other words, he disposes of time as decision, as choice, as the possibility of exploiting, subjugating, commanding, and managing other men. Money as purchasing power is, for Deleuze, that through which labor flows are reterritorialized and linked to consumption, family, employment, and subjection (worker, prof, man, women, etc.)—all the assignments of the social division of labor. Worker demands, as with most labor union politics, can thus be seen as a way of recognizing and accepting these subjections and power relations. On the other hand, worker demands and purchasing power may equally represent the breaking point of reterritorialization, the refusal of these subjections, provided that the wage flow derives from a flow of a different type, a different power. In the same way that capital must transform money (means of payment) into capital, the proletariat must transform the purchasing-power flow into a flow of autonomous and independent subjectivation, into a flow that interrupts the politics of capital, in order words, into a flow that is at once a refusal of and flight from the functions and subjections to which the proletariat has been confined. Capital has power over the purchasing-power flow of workers foremost because it controls the financing flow, it controls time, choice, and decision.[43] Money as capital has a power of destruction/creation that money as purchasing power does not.[44]

The flow of financing, that is, money as capital, is a mutant power, a creative flow, a set of "sign powers," because it engages the future, manifests a force of prescription, and constitutes a power of destruction/creation that anticipates that which is not yet present. Financing flows are a deterritorialized and deterritorializing power, a power that does not emerge after the economic but is immanent to it. They affect possibilities and their actualization.

The substance of money as capital is time, but less labor time than time as the possibility of choice, decision, and control, in other words, the power to destroy/create social forms of exploitation and subjection. Money as a means of payment, on the other hand, is a "powerless sign," since it functions solely as a means to acquire goods that already exist by establishing "a one-to-one relation between money and an imposed range of products."[45]

In purchasing power, "money represents a potential break-deduction on a [given] flow of consumption" (given power relations). In the financing structure money functions as a potential "break-detachment" which rearticulates chains of capital valorization and accumulation, reconfigures the composition of the labor force and the population, and establishes new forms of subjection. The specificity of capitalist power does not derive from the mere accumulation of purchasing power but from the capacity to reconfigure power relations and processes of subjectivation.[46]

We should note that in crises the recovery of damages due to money as capital ("virtual" money, since it remains to be fully actualized) depends on revenue money (wages and public spending, actual money).

By conceiving of money as deriving from debt and by asserting its infinite nature, joined to the infinite of "production for production's sake," Deleuze and Guattari grasped very early on and throughout their work one of the major transformations of modern-day capitalism. This brief history of debt ought to be complemented by a short history of taxes, since neoliberal policies are also, and inextricably, fiscal policies. Their analyses, which we cannot develop further here, are taken up especially in *Anti-Oedipus*.

Basing himself on the research of Edouard Will, Michel Foucault shows how, in certain Greek tyrannies, the tax on aristocrats and the distribution of money to the poor are a means of bringing the money back to the rich and a means of remarkably widening the regime of debts [...] (As if the Greeks had discovered in their own way what the Americans rediscovered after the New Deal: that heavy taxes are good for business.) In a word, money—the circulation of money—*is the means for rendering the debt infinite.* [...] [T]he abolition of debts or their accountable transformation initiates the duty of an interminable service to the State [...]. The infinite creditor and infinite credit have replaced the blocks of mobile and finite debts. [...] [D]ebt becomes a *debt of existence,* a debt of the existence of the subjects themselves. A time will come when the creditor has not yet lent while the debtor never quits repaying, for repaying is a duty but lending is an option—as in Lewis Carroll's song, the long song about the infinite debt:

> A man may surely claim his dues:
> But, when there's money to be lent,
> A man must be allowed to choose
> Such times as are convenient.[47]

We would like to stress the importance of a book like *Anti-Oedipus.* In it, the authors ventured onto the terrain that the capitalist power bloc had favored for its counter-revolution—by overturning May '68. Neoliberalism has since confirmed, through its management of debt, the nature of the 21st-century class struggle announced in *Anti-Oedipus*: the *univocity of production*, which affects the economy and subjectivity equally. The debt economy is an economy that requires a subject capable of accounting for himself as a future subject, a subject capable of promising and keeping a promise, a subject that works on the self. If classical political economy along with Marx located the essence of wealth in subjective activity irreducible to the sphere of representation, still, they were perhaps wrong to have it hinge on "labor." In any case, as we now better understand how the creditor-debtor relationship functions, it is time to examine exactly how it fits into the neoliberal economy and reconfigures the political and social sphere.

3

THE ASCENDENCY OF DEBT
IN NEOLIBERALISM

FOUCAULT AND THE "BIRTH" OF NEOLIBERALISM

Debt constitutes the most deterritorialized and the most general power relation through which the neoliberal power bloc institutes its class struggle. Debt represents a transversal power relation unimpeded by State boundaries, the dualisms of production (active/non-active, employed/unemployed, productive/non-productive), and the distinctions between the economy, the political, and the social. It immediately acts at the global level, affecting entire populations, calling for and contributing to the ethical construction of the indebted man.

How does this field of relations constructed by debt inhabit different mechanisms of power and different forms of subjectivation? To answer this question, we are going to join the theoretical tools we have recovered with Michel Foucault's theory of power, whose origin in Nietzsche, our own starting point, Foucault recognized explicitly. How has debt, since the 1970s, reconfigured sovereign, disciplinary, and biopolitical power?

In his important book on neoliberalism, *The Birth of Biopolitics*, Foucault, setting aside what he had argued in the course mentioned above on the functions of money in ancient Greece, neglects the functions of finance, debt, and money, even though these constituted the strategic mechanisms of neoliberal government starting in the late 1970s. Indeed, the debt economy appears just as much in geopolitical areas (Southeast Asia, South America, Europe) as among national populations (Argentina, Greece, Ireland, Spain, Portugal, etc.). It provides leverage in most social conflicts; its power is exercised on individuals (family debt), thereby embodying the point of view of the "collective capitalist." We note in passing that the transformation of capitalism and its money occurring in the late 1970s did not, however, escape Deleuze, who summed up the transition from disciplinary governance to contemporary neoliberalism in this way: "A man is no longer a man confined [as in disciplinary societies] but a man in debt [in a control society]."[1]

For Foucault, neoliberals no longer conceive *homo economicus* as the subject of exchange and the market but as an entrepreneur (of the self). Foucault's description of the neoliberal practices implemented in order to transform the worker into "human capital" is at once quite enlightening and misleading. The worker, on his own initiative, is supposed to guarantee the formation, growth, accumulation, improvement, and valorization of the "self" as "capital." No doubt the "worker" is no longer considered solely as a mere factor of production; he is no longer, properly speaking, a labor force, but a skill-capital, a "skill-machine," which goes hand in hand with a "lifestyle, a way of life," an "entrepreneurial" ethical position that creates "a form of relationship of the individual to himself, time, those around him, the group, and the family."[2]

Nonetheless, this injunction to make the individual "a sort of permanent and complex enterprise" occurs within a context—that of the debt economy—completely different from that described by Foucault. The perspective of *The Birth of Biopolitics* is thus still that of the German Ordoliberals for whom the industrial firm and entrepreneur were at the heart of the "social market economy." Foucault remained attached to this "industrial" view of postwar neoliberalism at a time when, throughout the 1970s, a logic of business—financialized business—became the norm. With it came a capitalism whose collective interest is represented by financial entrepreneurs who have imposed a new "government of conduct" and a new kind of individualization, which have little to do with postwar Ordoliberal politics. As Foucault suggests, neoliberal government must always act on society itself, by taking charge of social processes in order to make room within them for competition and business as well as and above all (here, a paramount distinction) for debt and the debt economy.

Ordoliberals advocated for an economic and social politics whose main objective was the "deproletarianization" of the population (the creation of small production units, property-ownership assistance, worker shareholders, etc.). The latter was supposed to ward off the political danger posed by large industrial firms in which the proletariat could organize and become an autonomous political force, which was the case from the late 19th century to the beginning of the 20th. A large portion of these "deproletarianization" policies were enacted through the Welfare State and through business co-management structures. The latter made a genuine transfer of wealth to workers possible while involving them in the capitalist management of society: "a wage-earner who is also a capitalist is no longer a proletarian"— and that, regardless of the "growing 'salarization' of the economy." In contemporary neoliberalism, deproletarianization has taken a leap forward in terms of discourse ("everyone an owner, everyone an entrepreneur"), but it has been transformed into its opposite in fact, namely because of wage depression and State budget cuts. This is how the debt economy institutes economic and existential precariousness, which is but the new name for the old reality: proletarianization—especially of the middle class and the class of workers in those new fields of what was once called, before the bubble burst, the "new economy."

The economy of debt provides a clearer picture of the capital's new subjective types to which the whole of the population is made to correspond. The picture is quite different from the one announced by the new economy of the 1980s and 1990s as well as from that described by Foucault.

Even though neoliberalism equally involves the economy and subjectivity, "work" and "work on the self," it reduces the latter to an injunction to become one's own boss, in the sense of "taking upon oneself" the costs and risks that business and the State externalize onto society. The promise of what "work on the self" was supposed to bring to "labor" in terms of emancipation (plea-sure, self-fulfillment, recognition, experimentation with different forms of life, mobility, etc.) has been rendered void, transformed into the impera-tive to take on the risks and costs that neither business nor the State are willing to undertake. By capping wages (through wage deflation) and by drastically reducing public spending, today's neoliberal policies produce human capital and "entrepreneurs of the self" who are more or less in debt, more or less poor, but in any case always precarious. For the majority of the population, becoming an entrepreneur of the self is restricted to managing, according to the terms of business and competition, its employability, its debts, the drop in wages and income, and the reduction of public services. With the new social welfare system in France, for example, "managerial" skills are demanded of the poor so that they are able to handle the many responsibilities of "assistance" and menial jobs. It then becomes unnecessary to create one's own small business in order to become an entrepreneur; one need only behave like one, adopt the same logic, the attitudes, the ways of relating to the world, to oneself, and to others.

Since the financial crisis following the dot-com bubble, capitalism has abandoned the epic narratives it constructed around the supposed freedom, innovation, and creativity of the entrepreneur, the knowledge society, etc. Now the population has only to worry itself with what finance, corporations, and the Welfare State "externalize" onto society—period!

The independence and freedom that entrepreneurism was supposed to bring to "labor" have in reality led to a greater and more intense dependence not only on institutions (business, the State, finance), but also on the self. This independence might ironically be considered the economy's colonization of the Freudian superego, since the "ideal self" can no longer be limited to the role of custodian and guarantor of the "morals" and values of society. In addition and above all, it must be the custodian and guarantor of the individual's productivity. We always come back to the coupling of economics and ethics, work and work on the self. The ferocious critique leveled in *Anti-Oedipus* against Freudian and Lacanian psychoanalysis can be read as anticipating the expansion of the "cure" and "analyst/analysand" transference to the management of the labor force in the corporation and to the population in society at large. The increase in psychologists', sociologists', and other "self-help" experts' interventions, the creation of "coaching" for better-off workers and obligatory individual monitoring for the poor and unemployed, the explosion of "care of the self" techniques in society—these are symptoms of the new forms of individual government, which include, above all, the shaping of subjectivity.

Before exploring how the debt economy forms subjectivity, we need to return in some detail to the changes the debt economy makes to the organization of power and the economy at a more general level in contemporary societies. This will allow us to understand how the economy of debt has radically transformed our possibilities for action both at a subjective and collective level.

DEBT'S RECONFIGURATION OF SOVEREIGN, DISCIPLINARY, AND BIOPOLITICAL POWER

In what way do the debt economy and the creditor-debtor relationship intersect with one of the most important and innovative categories of power established by Foucault? Although providing a remarkable real-time analysis of the rise of neoliberalism, Foucault was only able to anticipate in part the reconfiguration of sovereign, disciplinary, and biopolitical power it would operate.

Sovereign Power

The debt economy first reconfigures the sovereign power of the State by neutralizing and undermining one of its regal prerogatives, monetary sovereignty, that is, the power of destruction/creation of money. In the 1970s, "finance" began the process of privatizing money, the source of all privatizations. We remind the reader that to protect the privatization of money imperiled by the 2007 financial crisis, neoliberals did not hesitate to raise the prospect of "nationalizing" losses, nationalizations—the State seizure of market freedom—which they viewed with absolute horror.

Finance has appropriated most of the functions of bank money to such an extent that central bank policies are strongly determined by the financial sector's demand for liquidity. Bank money, money that exists mostly on a computer screen, is issued by private banks based on a debt—a debt that then becomes its intrinsic nature such that it is also called "debt-money" or "credit money." It is not attached to any material standard, nor does it refer to any substance except for the debt relation itself. In this way, with bank money, not only does one produce debt, but money itself is "debt" and no more than a power relation between creditor and debtor. In the euro zone, the issuance of private debt/money represents 92.1% of all the money in circulation in the largest money aggregate.

Monetary sovereignty also has to compete with finance. Securities negotiated on the stock market represent an "incipient form of money." "Their liquidity is only partial [but] their circulation is already surprisingly vast, not only as a means of reserve, but also as a means of exchange for certain transactions."[3] As Marazzi suggests, starting in the 1990s, the money supply developed independently of any kind of quantitative objective set by the central monetary authorities. National central banks restricted themselves to answering the demand for liquidity. The "independence" of the Central Bank with regard to Treasury is, in reality, a mask for its dependence on the markets.

During the same period, a new power bloc formed based on the debt economy, uniting what continues stubbornly to be taken separately: the so-called "real" economy, the "financial" economy, and the State. The State deliberately transferred its prerogative of creating money to the "private" sector. Contrary to what the vast majority of economists, experts, and journalists maintain, there is in fact no competition or conflict between State financial and monetary policy, but a new neoliberal alliance bringing together banks, institutional investors, private enterprise, governments, entire swaths of public administration, as well as the media and academics, etc.—an alliance that has systematically taken aim at the logic of the Welfare State and social spending. If there is any conflict, it is between two conceptions of the State and State monetary and social policy. But the neoliberal bloc came out on top long ago and now holds a hegemonic position within the economy, public administration, the State, political parties, business, and the media. This new bloc of power would never have seen the light of day without the help of public authorities (governments on the right as well as the left—in France, essentially Socialist governments—States, and central banks). And as the latest financial crisis has shown, the State (as "lender of last resort") enables the reproduction of capitalist power relations founded on debt.

It has been remarked that, contrary to theories of the decline of nation-states, their number has in fact increased rather than diminished with the rise of neoliberalism. But that misses the point, since what has changed are the functions of the nation-state, the ways in which it intervenes, and its purpose. It is nonetheless surprising to see how States and governments never fail to dance to the ratings agencies' tune, whether in Greece, Ireland, Iceland, Portugal (where the governments fell), Spain, Italy, or the UK—and that is only the most recent financial crisis. The agencies are in the service of the financial power bloc and represent one of its strategic weapons. Ratings agencies, financial investors,[4] and institutions like the IMF have thus been able to seriously undermine State sovereign power. European States now have no choice but to apply the economic and social policies dictated by the markets (that is, by the economic-political-financial power bloc) based on the new European stability pact. Elections in these countries take place against a backdrop of economic programs already determined by the economic and financial constraints imposed on them from outside the national territory.

Disciplinary Power

Having examined how the debt economy reconfigures State sovereign power, it is now necessary to look at how the debt economy reconfigures the most important disciplinary power described by Foucault, following Marx—that of private enterprise. Indeed, the debt economy revives Keynes's euthanasia of the rentier by reestablishing like never before in the history of capitalism the power of the shareholder over all other company actors, especially its workers. Owners of capital securities, along with managers, who are themselves transformed into shareholders, are the only ones to benefit from gains in productivity.

Finance has thus put in place a business "government" whose general principles are the following: "The primacy of the shareholder over the director of the company; the subordination of company management to shareholder interests; in the case of conflicts of interest, the primacy of the shareholder."[5] Finance dictates to and imposes on private firms a new "measure" of value, implemented through new international accounting standards, called IFRS (International Financial Reporting Standards), developed in the exclusive interest of investors and shareholders and in force since January 1, 2005, in all listed European corporations. The new accounting is supposed to allow for comparisons between companies' financial performance at any point in time and for any business sector.

> The accounting standards consider the company to be a financial asset whose value is determined by the market. [...] Only the joint stock company (an SA corporation, for example) has a legal existence. On the other hand, the law does not recognize the economic company, in the sense of an entity that produces goods and services. Company actors other than the shareholders, notably, the workers, are not considered owners of the wealth produced, even if they contribute to it directly.[6]

Shareholders and financial institutions decide, control, and prescribe the forms of valorization, the accounting procedures, the salary levels, the organization of labor, the pace, and the productivity of the company.

The contractualization of "social relations" is another "innovation" finance has imposed. First within companies and for several years now within "public services," it has been part of a process of individualization that aims to neutralize "collective" logics. Even with unemployment insurance and welfare assistance, beneficiaries are made to sign an "individual contract" in order to claim their right to compensation. The company, then, is not a place of conflict between workers and bosses, nor are public services a place where highly asymmetrical powers are exercised between agents representing the administration and beneficiaries (the unemployed, the sick, welfare recipients). The private firm or public institution is a set of *individual contracts* linking different actors who, in the pursuit of their own individual interest, are all equal.

There is, therefore, no contradiction but a *convergence* between what one persists in calling the real economy and the virtual economy. A large part of company revenue is made up of financial revenue. Investments in financial products by non-financial companies have risen more quickly than their so-called productive investments in machinery or the labor force. Companies' dependence on financial revenue continues to increase. "With the tendency toward the financialization of the non-financial economy, not only is the manufacturing sector quantitatively dominant, but it is in fact the sector that drives the process." This is all that is needed, Christian Marazzi argues, for the distinction between the real economy and the financial economy to disappear completely, just as we must stop identifying capitalism with industrial capitalism alone, both from a theoretical and historical point of view.

Biopolitical Power

Finally, the politics of debt have come to completely pervade what Foucault calls biopower. The former is not limited to making public spending the source of new profits for creditors (insurance and institutional investors), but transforms the very nature of the Welfare State. The "collective" insurance against risks (old age, illness, unemployment, etc.) has been systematically replaced by private insurance wherever possible.

By simultaneously reducing social spending and taxes (reductions that above all benefit business and the wealthiest segments of the population), neoliberal State policies have engaged a twofold process: a massive transfer of revenue to business and the wealthiest and an expansion of deficits due to fiscal policies, deficits which have in turn become a source of revenue for creditors buying State debt. The "virtuous circle" of the debt economy is thus complete. This has prompted Warren Buffet, the oracle of the American stock market, to admit with the honesty and lucidity particular to reactionaries: "Everything is going quite well for the rich in this country. We've never had it so good. It's a class war, and my class is winning." As far as the Welfare State is concerned, the strategic process of the neoliberal program consists in a progressive transformation of "social rights" into "social debts." Neoliberal policies in turn transform the latter into private debts, in parallel with the transformation of "beneficiaries" into "debtors" of unemployment insurance regimes (for the unemployed) and the State (for beneficiaries of welfare programs, etc.).

The transformation of social rights into debts and beneficiaries into debtors is part of a program of "patrimonial individualism," "whose basis is the assertion of individual rights, but according to a completely financial conception of these rights, rights understood as securities."[7] Unlike what happens on financial markets, the beneficiary as "debtor" is not expected to reimburse in actual money but rather in conduct, attitudes, ways of behaving, plans, subjective commitments, the time devoted to finding a job, the time used for conforming oneself to the criteria dictated by the market and business, etc. Debt directly entails life discipline and a way of life that requires "work on the self," a permanent negotiation with oneself, a specific form of subjectivity: that of the indebted man. In other words, debt reconfigures biopolitical power by demanding a production of subjectivity specific to indebted man.

In this way, by reconfiguring sovereign, disciplinary, and biopolitical power, the debt economy fulfills at once political, productive, and distributive functions.

What Is Capitalism?

Having looked at how the debt economy reconfigures different forms of power, we must now
turn more specifically to how power is exercised
within capitalism. What does the debt economy
mean and what relationship does it establish
between financial capital, industrial capital, and
the State? Can we speak of the hegemony of financial
capitalism over other forms of capital (industrial,
commercial)? These are formidable questions, whose
terms may not be the best.

It is useless to look for a foundation of what
goes by the name of capitalism (industry, finance,
the State, or even knowledge production), since
there is no single site from which power relations
emerge; there is no single place, institution, one
mechanism more strategic than the others, in
which capitalist power might be accumulated and
from which transformations—whether neoliberal
or revolutionary—might be effectuated. There is
no one type of relation (economic, political, debt,
knowledge) capable of containing, totalizing, and
dominating the others. Every economic, political,
or social mechanism produces effects of power
specific to it, requires specific tactics and strategies,

and affects the "governed" according to different processes of subjection and subjugation [*asservissement*]. But how, then, is it possible to speak of the debt economy at all? What I am calling the debt economy is an arrangement that holds this multiplicity together. The unity is not systemic but operational, that is to say that it constitutes a "politics" which gives rise to always partial and temporary compositions and unifications. In any case, within capitalism, "politics" is always defined relative to the priorities and imperatives of class conflict.

The need to respond to and move beyond the power relations that crystallized around May '68 has led to the creation of a power bloc acting— often by trial and error—on different mechanisms of power at the same time (at times favoring the market, at others business or the State). But the underlying framework connecting these mechanisms has been the creditor-debtor relationship, which has not always had the same influence or the same function but has in practice shown itself to be the most useful and effective. The crisis of 2007 increased its usefulness and effectiveness even more in the eyes of the neoliberal power bloc, for it combined the "extraction of surplus value" and control of the population at a breadth and depth of which industrial capitalism is incapable. The creditor-debtor relationship is most effective for dealing with crises in the liberal dynamic, since it brings the issue of property to the fore. For all that, are we really talking about hegemony? The Gramscian concept of "hegemony" (the hegemony of financial capital) seems less relevant here than Foucault's "governmentality."

Capitalism is not a *structure* or a *system*: it develops, transforms, plans, integrates more or less well-adapted procedures according to imperatives of exploitation and domination. The power of capitalism, like the world it aims to appropriate and control, is always *in the process of being made*. The power bloc amassed around the debt economy is constituted through power relations that are at once heterogeneous—because responding to different logics (the State with its sovereign functions, Welfare State control of the population; industry and its capital accumulation through labor; finance, which claims to have no need of labor; the political, which creates consensus, etc.)—and complementary, because the power bloc faces a common "enemy." The class struggle unites and consolidates these relations or splits and weakens them. Their unity and internal power relations are part of a political process in composition that cannot be taken a priori.

Governmentality has produced a collective capitalist—as Lenin would put it—which is not concentrated in finance, but operates throughout business, administration, service industries, political parties, the media, and the university. This political subjectivation provides capitalists with the same education, the same vision of the economy and society, the same vocabulary, the same methods, in short, the same politics. Although neoliberal governmentality is undoubtedly based on debt, which encompasses the other power relations in an increasingly problematic way, its development must be historicized, since, in moving from one political moment to another, its form changes. The governmentality Foucault describes in *The Birth of Biopolitics* does not seem sufficient for understanding what it implies from the 1990s on, when governmentality began to limit the freedom which Foucault made the condition of "liberalism." The freedom in liberalism is always and primarily the freedom of private ownership and owners. When the "rights of man" are threatened—by a crisis, a revolt, or some other phenomenon—regimes of governmentality other than liberal governmentality are required in order to ensure their durability. In this way, the problem of "governing as little as possible" first created the conditions for, then gave way to, as has always been the case in the history of capitalism, ever more authoritarian politics. To read *The Birth of Biopolitics* in the light of what is taking place today is to be struck by a certain political naiveté, since the parable of "liberalism" always describes, leads to, the same thing: crisis, limitations on democracy and "liberal" freedoms, and the institution of more or less authoritarian regimes according to the intensity of the class struggle to wage in order to maintain the "privileges" of private property.

We must therefore examine pragmatically and historically the function of different power relations, asking ourselves not what capitalism is but how it functions with regard to the class struggle, which only the great reactionaries, like Warren Buffet, talk about with any relevance.

The Subprime Crisis

This is why the current crisis is not only a financial crisis but also a failure of neoliberal governmentality of society. The mode of government founded on business and proprietary individualism has failed. By revealing the nature of power relations, the crisis has led to much more "repressive" and "authoritarian" forms of control, which no longer bother with the rhetoric of the 1980s and 1990s of greater "freedom," creativity, and wealth.

The genealogy and development of the subprime crisis uncovers how the power bloc functions, how the "real" economy, finance, and the State represent the moving parts of the same mechanism and the same political project—what we have called the debt economy. Here again, the "real" economy and financial "speculation" are inseparable. Whereas the "real" economy impoverishes the governed as "wage-earners" (through wage freezes, precarization, etc.) and possessors of social rights (through narrower income redistribution, decreases in social services, unemployment insurance, and student grants, etc.), finance claims to enrich them through credit and stock. No direct or indirect wage hikes (pensions); instead, consumer credit and the push for stock market investment (pension funds, private insurance). No right to housing; instead, real estate loans. No right to tuition; instead, university loans. No risk mutualization (unemployment, health, retirement, etc.); instead, investment in private insurance.

The wage-earner and the beneficiary of public programs must earn and spend as little as possible in order to reduce labor costs and the costs of public services, whereas the consumer must spend as much as possible in order to use up production. But in modern-day capitalism, the worker, the beneficiary, and the consumer are all one and the same. This is where finance steps in to resolve the paradox. Neoliberal economic growth creates ever greater disparities in income and power by impoverishing workers, public assistance beneficiaries, and a portion of the middle class, while simultaneously aiming to make them rich through a mechanism best exemplified by subprime credit: income redistribution that leaves profits untouched; redistribution while reducing taxes (above all for business and the rich); redistribution while cutting into wages and social spending. With declines in wages and the destruction of the Welfare State, credit is the only solution if everyone is to get rich. How does this kind of politics function? "You don't make much money? Not a problem! Take out loans to buy a house, its value will increase, and that will serve as collateral on new loans." But once interest rates rise, the whole mechanism of income "distribution" through debt and financing collapses.

The logic of debt/credit is a political logic for governing social classes within globalization. The way subprimes have worked offers a paradigmatic example.

The boom in real estate and easy credit were two ways to pacify workers and the middle class and make them go along with the long-term program of the "liberal system." When we wanted to buy a house, a car, or a vacation to Paris on credit, we were made to believe in the success of globalization. Now people are beginning to realize that this was a Wall Street strategy for robbing them of everything they owned. Now they don't know where to turn, because their house was their last reserve in case of an emergency.[8]

The American economy is fundamentally a debt economy. Within it finance does not primarily represent speculation but rather is the driver and determines the nature of growth. On June 30, 2008, the aggregate US debt—for families, businesses, banks, and government—exceeded $51 trillion, compared to a GDP of $14 trillion. In the US, the average household debt increased by 22% over the eight years under George W. Bush. The amount of unpaid loans rose by 15%. Student debt doubled. Learning how to "live with debt" has now been made part of certain American school curricula.

Demand no longer increases by and large through State deficits but through private debt, which unloads the costs and risks on "indebted" families. Over the last several years, their debt has been a major contributing factor to the rise and expansion of finance. And lest we forget, real estate loans set off the latest financial crisis. In other words, as Christian Marazzi argues, we have moved from public deficit spending to private deficit spending in order to prop up the global demand for goods and services. The public deficit has not, of course, disappeared, especially in the US, where income taxes are largely insufficient to offset the growth in public spending. However, global demand has been maintained through financial markets and banks, as in the case of subprime loans.

Finance is a war machine for privatization, which transforms social debt into credit, into individual insurance, and rent (shareholders) and, thus, individual property. Stop by your bank: finance has discovered the most ingenious techniques for transforming everyone into credit-card wielding owners and consumers. "Speculation" has not failed, nor the supposed uncoupling of finance and the real economy, but the claim that everyone can get rich without affecting the private property regime. Property is the stumbling block of all capitalist politics: *hic Rhodus, hic salta*! At this level, the class struggle manifests itself in the opposition between two models of wealth "socialization": rights for all and mutualized risks and costs versus individual credit and insurance. What has failed is the political project of transforming everyone into "human capital" and entrepreneurs of the self. With the subprime market, capitalists believed in their own ideology of transforming everyone into "owners," even the poorest of the working and middle classes. "Everyone an owner!" proclaimed Sarkozy's election platform in 2007, borrowing from Bush's proclamation of an "ownership society." What has proved true, however, is that the majority of the population has been converted into debtors and a minority into rentiers. The failure of proprietary individualism brings the debt economy to the fore as well as the least pleasant aspect of the creditor-debtor relationship: repayment.

The objectives of the debt economy are thoroughly political: the neutralization of collective attitudes (mutualization, solidarity, cooperation, rights for all, etc.) and the memory of the collective struggles, action, and organization of "wage-earners" and the "proletariat." Growth gained on credit (finance) aims to diffuse the conflict. Having to confront subjectivities that consider public assistance, retirement, education, etc., as collective rights guaranteed by past struggle is not the same thing as governing "debtors," small business owners, and minor shareholders.

The subprime crisis is thus not solely a financial crisis. It also marks the failure of the political program of proprietary and patrimonial individualism. The crisis is highly symbolic in that it strikes at the emblem par excellence of "individual property": home ownership. In the short term, the failure of neoliberal politics provides the occasion for the power bloc instituted by the debt economy to benefit from the crisis in which the whole world now finds itself.

Who is going to pay the mountains of debt piled up to save the banks and the system of power of the debt economy? The response coming from the neoliberal power bloc could not be clearer. Yet it relies on a strategy over which the neoliberal sorcerer's apprentices may not have any control.

The Sovereign Debt Crisis

The debt problem is still very much with us. It has only shifted from private debt to sovereign State debt. The enormous sums that States have handed over to banks, insurance companies, and institutional investors must now be "reimbursed" by the taxpayers (and not by the shareholders and purchasers of stock). The highest costs will be borne by wage-earners, beneficiaries of public programs, and the poorest of the population.

Banks were saved through the use of "public" money to nationalize their losses. The State injected a money flow into society—which is, as Deleuze has shown us, a flow of power—in order to reestablish and reinforce the power relation between creditors and debtors. States have not rescued a functional structure of real economy financing, but rather a mechanism for domination and exploitation specific to modern-day capitalism. And, in a cynical turn, the costs of reestablishing this relation of exploitation and domination will have to be paid for by its victims.

A new political moment has begun whose consequences are impossible to foresee. The drive to profit from the crisis in order to fully accomplish the neoliberal program (by reducing wages to subsistence levels, reducing public spending, transforming the Welfare State, accelerating privatizations) is risky for Capital because it weakens the State, a fundamental structure for political control and the formation of subjectivity. It also energizes the class struggle. Believing their own rhetoric, according to which the market can do without the State, ratings agencies opened hostilities when they revealed their attack on sovereign debt (Europe's first of all). By putting States on the verge of default, the agencies have compelled deficit countries to impose the social and wage policies which neoliberals have dreamed of since the 1970s. Because "there is no choice," creditors, already fattened on forty years' worth of preying on public debt, will have to be reimbursed. After having lowered wages, Greece, in 2010, moved back the retirement age, froze pensions, increased the VAT, and implemented, under orders from Europe and the IMF, a second economic plan. The latter, adding austerity to austerity, forecasts 6 billion euros in savings in 2011, 26 billion from 2012 to 2015, privatizations (electricity, the lottery, Athens's former airport, ports, marinas) coming to 50 billion euros, an additional two and a half hours to the work week, and the elimination of 200,000 public sector jobs. In 2010, 120,000 stores closed, in 2011, 6,000 restaurants, whose clientele had already dropped by 54% on average. Everything worth anything must go. That revenue drops proportionally for the State budget does not seem to worry the IMF nor that bastion of neoliberalism, Europe. The only thing that matters is that creditors are repaid (and above all German and French banks, which, because they hold Greek debt obligations, will be saved with "public" money for a second time). To ensure that the program works, the sale of all these assets will be under the close scrutiny, if not the control, of foreign experts. Under the new "assistance" plan, Greek debt went from 150 to 170% of GDP.[9] European and IMF rescue plans are also in the process of plunging Ireland into a recession with no end in sight.

In an interview in *La Stampa* on July 9, 2011, the American economist John Coffee discussed Italy's public debt, which had just fallen prey to market attacks, and what lay behind the Greek rescue. In response to a question regarding Italian debt, whose obligations are held in large part by Italian "families," that is, by small and very small savers, he remarked:

In absolute terms, it is true that if the debt is in the hands of actual families, that offers some stability. But we are in a phase where Greek risks default and the European Central Bank wants to avoid it in order to save the French and German banks that would suffer the fallout. If, on the other hand, Italy were to default, most of the weight would fall on families and not on European banks. This might push the ECB to help Greece more than Italy. The markets are well aware of this and behave accordingly.

The markets are well aware of it, whereas journalists, it seems, are not. Can we even imagine what would happen if the media had the courage to say the truth, replacing every "Greek rescue" with "French and German bank rescue"? Things would be happening within an entirely different political framework.

Portugal, after four austerity plans in one year to try to escape European and IMF rescue plans, which impose conditions, as Brazilian ex-president Lula recently recalled, that make problems worse rather than better, ended up having to accept $80 billion in aid which it immediately disbursed among its French, Spanish, and German creditors (banks), which hold the lion's share of its debt. As for Icelanders, they will have to pay 12,000 euros per person for one private bank's default. The only citizens to have been asked by referendum, they twice refused the austerity plans proposed.

The British government has implemented an austerity plan that looks to reduce public spending by 81 billion pounds (92.7 billion euros) by 2015, which means an average drop of 28% for local community budgets over the period. In those European countries which the ratings agencies have yet to descend upon, and even in countries like Germany, austerity plans figured in the billions of euros have been put in place, affecting workers, incomes, and ways of life especially among the most vulnerable.

But it is in the US, the epicenter of the crisis and the cradle of neoliberalism, that neoconservative politicians are threatening to make the most of the financial crisis by following the neoliberal logic to the end. The Democrat Barack Obama boasts of having negotiated the largest cut in public spending ever made in the US, as if he were priding himself on signing a new New Deal, only in reverse. In November 2010, he made an agreement with the majority-Republican Congress to prolong by two years the tax cuts George W. Bush had given to the wealthiest Americans. The Bush-Obama law extends the tax cuts even to those making more than $250,000. The income bracket represents only 5% of the population, whereas their taxes account for more than 40% of income tax revenue.

In exchange for peanuts for the unemployed, the rich received $315 billion over two years. To have an idea of the size of the handout, one should remember that the US government investment in the economy came to $800 billion in 2008, the highest level in the country's history. Neo-conservatives are having a high time drastically reducing "welfare" spending at the state level as they wait to do the same at the federal level. In a recent book, Arianna Huffington reminds us that such cuts are already law in forty-five states.[10] In February, 2011, over the course of three days thousands descended on Madison, Wisconsin, to protest the proposals of the new Republican governor, Scott Walker. He had been elected on the promise of reducing deficits while lowering taxes at the same time. His plan was supposed to allow the state to save $300 million over the next two years (the state's budget deficit is around $5.4 billion). The debt reduction plan included a partial freeze on state-employee wages, a drop in employee pensions as well as in other social services, and the elimination of union organizing rights, which is not the least of austerity plan objectives the world over.

The negotiations over the debt ceiling between Democrats and Republicans looked like a carica-ture—though unfortunately a very real one—of the struggle between social classes in the US.

Conservatives refuse to touch the scandalous tax cuts on the wealthy and businesses and want to reduce the deficit through savage cuts on public spending, in other words, they want to apply to the federal budget what is already happening in states around the country.

Since the early 2000s France has quickly made up the ground it had lost to the US with regard to fiscal policies favoring the rich (especially the richest of the rich)[11] and corporations. The debate in spring 2011 about welfare assistance and the wealth tax is another version of the class struggle carried out through fiscal and social policies, with the aim of enforcing a "double penalty" on beneficiaries of welfare assistance (400 euros per month). Blamed for their situation, the latter are supposed to respect the "duties" imposed on them (the obligation to have their cases monitored, to accept any reasonable employment after two refusals, etc.) and, furthermore, work for free, while the government cuts checks of several billion euros to those paying the wealth tax, cutting the rate for the richest by nearly three-quarters (from 1.8% to 0.5% on more than 17 million euros). Tax exemptions, another mechanism for "assisting" the wealthiest, represent between 60 and 80 billion euros per year, a handout with nothing asked in return, neither in terms of duties nor in terms of "socially useful work"—billions of euros which the least well-off will have to pay for.

Through sovereign debt, indebted man may end up becoming the most widespread economic-existential condition in the world. The blow to neoliberal governmentality from the subprime crisis will, in the short run, be transformed into a victory for the universal debt economy. It is therefore essential to see how, through the sovereign debt crisis, the logic of debt has come to pervade what Foucault called "the social."

Three Kinds of Debt: Private, Sovereign, and Social

During periods of crisis such as the one occurring right now, it is not hard to see what "confidence"—spoken about ad nauseam by politicians, economists, and experts—really means. It certainly has nothing to do with other people, oneself, or the world. Instead, it has to do with those mechanisms of power capable of reproducing and governing capitalist relations of exploitation and domination. In particular, it has to do with money and sovereign debt with the State standing guarantor of last resort of their continuity. Private money (debt) has shown for the umpteenth time that it can guarantee the reproduction and government of power relations solely through greed, privatization, and the exploitation of every physical, intellectual, and ethical resource. If it does anything at all, the State does nothing to reestablish confidence but rather "security," which the State alone can guarantee.

Coordinating private debt always requires the intervention of State transcendence. In the final analysis, it is sovereign debt and not the market that makes possible and guarantees the circulation of private debt. The privatization of money thus inevitably leads to what market liberals are supposedly horrified of—namely, State intervention. That is what the current crisis reveals: the private issuance of credit money has required the State to intervene, since private debt is incapable of immanent coordination (self-regulation of the market). And it is at this point that something surprising has happened, which demonstrates the "madness" of capitalism. Sovereign debt has become the target of speculation and exploitation on the part of creditors and their representatives, who have sought to systematically destroy the very visible hand that saved them. We would be the last to lament the "madness" undermining one of the mainstays of control over the population—the nation-State and its administration. From one financial crisis to the next, we have now entered a period of permanent crisis, which we shall call "catastrophe" to refer to the discontinuity of the concept of crisis itself.

With money and credit, then, we rediscover the impasses of capitalism described by Foucault in *The Birth of Biopolitics*. In order to govern the heterogeneity of both the economic and political spheres, a third element, a third point of reference, is needed: the social. The political power of the sovereign, according to Foucault, is exercised within a territory and over subjects of right, a territory also inhabited by economic subjects, who, instead of having rights, have (economic) interests. *Homo economicus* is a heterogeneous figure that *homo juridicus* cannot completely account for. Economic man and the subject of right involve two radically different constitutional processes: every subject of right becomes integrated into a political community through a dialectics of renunciation, since political constitution presupposes that the legal subject transfer his rights to someone else. Economic man, on the other hand, becomes integrated into the economic whole through a spontaneous proliferation of his interests, all of which he retains. Indeed, it is only by maintaining his own selfish interest that everyone's needs can be met. According to Foucault, neither legal theory, nor economic theory, neither law, nor the market is capable of reconciling this heterogeneity. Another domain, another field, a new system of reference is needed that is neither the entirety of subjects of right nor the entirety of economic subjects. In order for governmentality to conserve its global character, in order for it not to split into two branches (the art of governing economically and the art of governing juridically), liberalism has invented and implemented a set of techniques for government it applies within a whole new system of reference: civil society, society, or the social. Society is supposed to be the aim of this great mechanism which reached its height of development in "welfare." In order to govern, the Welfare State must be introduced between the economy and the political system, and social rights must be introduced between political rights and economic interests.

Society is not the space in which a certain distance or a certain autonomy is created with respect to the State; rather, it is the correlate of governmental techniques. Society is not a primary and immediate reality but part of the modern technology of government, its product.

Debt operates in the same way. Between private debt and sovereign State debt, "social debt" (the Welfare State) must be introduced, a debt whose management, through what Foucault describes as a technique of "pastoral" control, makes it possible to individualize the government of behavior and totalize the regulation of the population. This is how processes of subjectivation, which we are now going to explore, and the more macroeconomic aspects of the debt economy are linked, and why it has seemed to us indispensable to consider them together. It is especially important to do so given that the failure of neoliberal governmentality brought on by the latest economic and financial crisis will undoubtedly intensify the debt economy's investment of the social sphere in Western societies.

Accordingly, the organization of the market, the State, and the social, which defines the government of society for Foucault, corresponds to the organization of the three kinds of debt which define the government of money/debt: private debt, sovereign debt, and social debt (the debt of the Welfare State). In order for governmentality to work, individualizing and totalizing management of social debt must be introduced between the polarizations capitalism continuously reproduces (the individualism of the market and the collectivism of the State, the freedom of the individual and the totalizing freedom of the State, etc.). Events occurring since the 1990s and greatly accelerating over the 2000s reveal a gap in Foucault's thinking in *The Birth of Biopolitics*, however. In the current crisis, the heterogeneity between *homo economicus* and *homo juridicus* is no longer maintained by the "social" but by the production of *homo debitor* (indebted man).

To convert the production of the social into the production of indebted man, changes must be made in the Welfare State, which is what the power bloc built around a politics of debt has been attempting to do for the last forty years. Here again, the theoretical tools we now have in our arsenal help us to grasp what the production of indebted man implies. Since the start of the latest financial crisis, we have seen a decisive turn in such a direction. The battles that once were fought over wages are now being fought over debt, and especially public debt, which represents a kind of socialized wage. Indeed, neoliberal austerity policies are concentrated in and fundamentally implemented through restrictions on all social rights (retirement, health care, unemployment, etc.), reductions in public services and employment, and wages for public workers—all for the purpose of constituting indebted man.

The production of the social through "welfare" used to act as an instrument for control over the lives of beneficiaries and as a means of reforming income redistribution and access to myriad services and rights. At present, the reformist route is blocked; only control remains, exercised through a politics of debt. From a means of capitalist reform, the Welfare State has become a means by which to establish authoritarian regimes. The function of the Welfare State has thus completely changed. Under these circumstances, a new New Deal is quite simply impossible. There is no question of economic equilibrium or economic imperatives, but rather of a politics of totalization and individualization of authoritarian control over indebted man. It is this fact that explains why it is impossible to return to reformist capitalism.

Hypocrisy, Cynicism, and Distrust in the Techniques of Debt Subjectivation

The theories of Marx and Nietzsche which we have thus far put to use also prove quite effective in helping to explain the way in which the debt economy forms the processes of subjectivity production. On the one hand, it appropriates and transforms from within what Foucault calls pastoral power: "an art of conducting, directing, leading, guiding, taking in hand, and manipulating men, an art of monitoring them and urging them on step by step, an art with the function of taking charge of men collectively and individually throughout their life and at every moment of their existence."[12] We are going to trace these processes of control and subjectivity production that today's Welfare State institutions execute on beneficiaries (the unemployed, poor workers, and welfare recipients). On the other hand, evaluation, whose importance within the debt economy both Nietzsche and Marx recognized, has become an extremely effective governmental technique in every sphere—economic, social, as well as education (especially at the university level)—for classifying, hierarchizing, and dividing the governed. Earlier we examined "objective debt," how it functions systemically or machinically. Now we shall look at the effects of "subjective debt," of "existential" debt, on the behavior of the governed.

In the text from 1844 we have already looked at, Marx adds that the affective environment in which the relationship between creditor and debtor occurs in both public and private sectors is ruled by hypocrisy, cynicism, and distrust.

> Mutual dissimulation, hypocrisy and sanctimoniousness are carried to extreme lengths [...]. [O]wing to this completely nominal existence of money, counterfeiting cannot be undertaken by man in any other material than his own person, he has to make himself into counterfeit coin, obtain credit by stealth, by lying, etc., and this credit relationship—both on the part of the man who trusts and of the man who needs trust—becomes an object of commerce, an object of mutual deception and misuse.[13]

We find this same affective environment in the modern-day Welfare State. With neoliberalism, the creditor-debtor relationship redefines biopolitical power, since the Welfare State not only intervenes in the "biology" of the population (birth, death, illness, risks, etc.), it requires ethico-political work on the self, an individualization involving a mix of responsibility, guilt, hypocrisy, and distrust. When social rights (unemployment insurance, the minimum wage, healthcare, etc.) are transformed into social debt and private debt, and beneficiaries into debtors whose repayment means adopting prescribed behavior, subjective relations between "creditor" institutions, which allocate rights, and "debtors," who benefit from assistance or services, begin to function in a radically different way, just as Marx foresaw.

If the mnemotechnics neoliberal government puts in place are usually not as gory and cruel as those described by Nietzsche (torture, mutilation, etc.), their purpose remains the same: to construct memory, inscribe "guilt" in the mind and body, fear and "bad conscience" in the individual economic subject. In order for the power of debt over the subjectivity of the welfare user to have its effect, the logic of individual and collective rights must be replaced by a logic of credit (investments of human capital).

I came to understand this phenomenon in all its violence while doing research and activist work

with the Coordination des intermittents et précaires d'Île-de France (CIP) (Coordination of
Intermittent and Precarious Workers of Île-de-
France).[14] I have transcribed some remarks below
from the study groups carried out with intermittent
workers and welfare recipients that attest to the
end of an era of "social rights." The transformation
of unemployment compensation into debt is part
of a long process in which we have witnessed techniques for making a debtor "subject." Indeed,
rights are universal and automatic since they are
recognized socially and politically, but debt is
administered by evaluating "morality" and
involves the individual as well as the work on the
self which the individual must undertake. The
logic of debt now structures and conditions the
process of individualization, a constant of social
policies. Each individual is a particular case which
must be studied carefully, because, as with a loan
application, it is the debtor's future plans, his style
of life, his "solvency" that guarantees reimbursement of the social debt he owes. As with bank
credit, rights are granted on the basis of a personal
application, following review, after information
on the individual's life, behavior, and modes of
existence has been obtained. The individualization
carried out by credit institutions introduces
arbitrariness and chance, since everything is
indexed, not to general and equal standards, but

to the idiosyncrasies of each subjectivity. One intermittent worker described the process in the following way:

> The payment and amount of compensation are determined by my conduct at work (with a big dose of morality involved: a bonus for seniority, perseverance, consistency, "professionalism," etc.). My unemployment office "file" (where they figure out the compensation) is specially adapted to my "case"; they measure me out a custom-made suit and my case becomes more and more specific. It is an up-to-date, personal "profile." There is little possibility of getting back to some kind of common measure that would be clearly stated and the same for everyone.

The individualization carried out by institutions now involves "morality" by mobilizing the "self," since the debtor's future actions must be molded, his uncertain future established in advance. Future behavior and conduct must be structured and controlled. Within neoliberalism, what the institution judges, appraises, and measures is, in the end, the style of life of individuals, who must be made to conform to the conception of the "good life" of the economy. Evaluations reflect the modes of existence, the ways of being of those who judge and, thus, of the economy.[15] The following are short excerpts from the workshops we undertook with public assistance beneficiaries as part of our research. The focus of our meeting was the "individual interview" (a monthly appointment with a counselor who "follows" unemployment insurance recipients, actualizing what Foucault called "pastoral power"), which specifically targets beneficiaries' style of life, their modes of being.

> She once asked me what I was interested in or what I wanted to do with my life or why I had chosen to do what I had been doing and I turned the question around on her: "And you, why are you in social work?" Because I thought it was all going a bit too far; I didn't have to tell her whole my life story. [...] I think if she kept on going like that it had to do with the image she had of me, how she understood my situation: that I'm someone who hasn't found her way, her career, and that she has to help me better understand what's going on with me, because I have skills but I have to find my career path. I couldn't tolerate that kind of relationship where I had to justify myself, tell her my life story, and so I told her absolutely nothing. She must have thought I was crazy.

The relationship with the institution always comes down to the user's "self." It requires the user/debtor to constantly consider the "self," to negotiate and compete with oneself. As Nietzsche says, the main purpose of debt lies in its construction of a subject and a conscience, a self that believes in its specific individuality and that stands as guarantor of its actions, its way of life (and not only employment) and takes responsibility for them. The techniques used in the individual interviews, which intrude on one's private life, that which is most subjective, push the welfare recipient to examine his life, his plans, and their validity. The State and its institutions act on subjectivities, mobilize the "innermost depths of the human heart," in order to orient behavior.

> The skills assessments, for example, they ask you to do all the time—and whatever you might think it's supposed to be about, there is always a part of it that intrudes on your personal life. I know people who have done detailed skills assessments and despite being super geared toward finding a job, the exercise isn't for everyone. It's something you're not necessarily used to doing, a kind of assessment of your life where you start to ask yourself questions, you think about yourself, like a kind of invasion of privacy couched in really appalling language, but that still makes you think.

In "individual monitoring," one is expected to come clean. Once a month, those on public assistance must talk about themselves (or make a show of themselves) and justify what they are doing with their lives and their time. But even in the case where the recipient resists this invasion of privacy, the violence against his person and his subjectivity, he is no less troubled by the "work on the self" these institutions oblige him to undertake.

Within the system of debt, the individualization of Welfare State policies is no longer solely disciplinary, since it entails a detailed analysis of the ability to "repay," which is repeatedly assessed on an individual basis. It always implies a "moral" evaluation of the individual's actions and modes of life. Repayment will be made not in money but through the debtor's constant efforts to maximize his employability, to take a proactive role in his integration into the work or social environment, to be available and flexible on the job market. Debt repayment is part of a standardization of behavior that requires conformity to the life norms dictated by the institution. This "subjective" relation between the public sector worker and the public assistance recipient, rather than moving beyond fetishism by reestablishing the "relation of man to man" spoken of by Marx, reveals itself instead as the source and height of the cynicism and hypocrisy of our "financialized" society. Continuous cynicism and hypocrisy not only in relations between bankers and customers, but also in relations between the State and the users of social services. In the same way as credit turns trust into distrust, the Welfare State suspects all users, and especially the poorest, of being cheats, of living at society's expense by taking advantage of public assistance instead of working. Under the conditions of ubiquitous distrust created by neoliberal policies, hypocrisy and cynicism now form the content of social relations.

In the same way, according to Marx, as credit encroaches on the private life of the person who applies for it by "spying" on him, the Welfare State invites itself into individuals' private lives in order to control the users' existence:

> Here it is also glaringly evident that distrust is the basis of economic trust; distrustful calculation whether credit ought to be given or not; spying into the secrets of the private life, etc. [...] As regards government loans, the state occupies exactly the same place as the man does in the earlier example... Owing to the fact that in the credit system the moral recognition of a man, as also trust in the state, etc., take the form of credit, the secret contained in the lie of moral recognition, the immoral vileness of this morality, as also the sanctimoniousness and egoism of that trust in the state, become evident and show themselves for what they really are.[16]

"Spying into the secrets of the private life" of assistance applicants is what welfare agents increasingly do, since underlying their work is "distrust" of the poor, the unemployed, precarious workers, all the potential "cheats" and "profiteers."

Institutions are not satisfied with intruding into a person's private life, with monitoring recipients' behavior. They enter people's private lives physically. Through their functionaries, they *invite themselves* into homes in order to investigate recipients' styles of life: an agent shows up at a person's home, enters the apartment or house, inspects the rooms, the bathroom to check how many toothbrushes there are, asks to see the electricity and phone bills, rent receipts, asks about lifestyle, and above all checks if the person is living alone. Indeed, if a partner is present, the latter is supposed to provide for one's needs, and then public assistance is stopped.

Debt operates not only in the manipulation of enormous quantities of money, in sophisticated financial and monetary policies; it informs and configures techniques for the control and production of users' existence, without which the economy would not have a hold on subjectivity.

Evaluation and Debt

Out of those texts by Nietzsche and Marx examined earlier, another, eminently topical consideration comes to light. It is through debt that evaluation as a technique for governing behavior comes to takes hold, a technique that today is employed in every economic and social sphere.

Heterodox economics, which studies financial power, seems to confirm Nietzsche's and Marx's intuition. Unlike the opacity and secretiveness that characterizes the factory and industry, financial power is essentially a power of "public" evaluation, whose claim is to make all organizations transparent, to make visible and thus assessable (measurable) the relations and behavior of the actors in each institution, whether it is a corporation, unemployment insurance, medicine, or the university. The creditor-debtor relationship entails a radical change in the measure of value. We have moved from an objective measure to a subjective one, carried out through evaluation. Thus André Orléan's argument:

> The power of the market is the power of public evaluation [...]. Financial power is a power of influence which controls debtors by subjecting them to a certified judgment, which generates a great deal of publicity within the financial community [...]. From this perspective, we can go so far as to say that it is a power of opinion.[17]

André Orléan goes so far as to say that "power moves from production to evaluation, from labor to opinion."

Given this, it seems relevant to examine the supposedly public nature of financial evaluation. Ratings agencies' assessment of UNEDIC with which we began our essay shows us the limits of the concept of public evaluation. There is nothing democratic about it, since only the financial community is involved. Assessment is done solely by ratings agencies, which are paid by the businesses, banks, or institutions they rate. This entails a huge conflict of interest which no one seems the least troubled by. Ratings agencies are not independent assessment firms but are rather integral to the "credit power" bloc. The public space of financial evaluation is that of the new oligarchies whose methods are thoroughly antidemocratic, for they aim to replace and destroy what is left of "co-determination" (the equal shared management—unions and bosses—of welfare institutions) as it emerged in the 20th century, starting with the New Deal. Even after it degenerated into corporatism, co-determination represented a rough attempt at institutional "social democracy." Since then, it has ossified under the debilitating monopoly of owner and worker unions. And while it has unhesitatingly opened up to the judgment and assessments of finance, it still refuses to consider those primarily concerned (the unemployed, welfare users, citizens). In order for social evaluation to be democratic, other authorities, other democratic mechanisms must see the light of day—mechanisms other than those involved in the corporatism of union-backed co-determination supported by financial power.

The rise of financial evaluation represents in practice an expropriation and deprivation of the power to act. Indeed, the increase in management techniques based on evaluation has narrowed the space left to wage-earners, users, and the governed in general to understand what is going on, to choose, and to decide. This state of affairs is particularly obvious in trades and professions still today considered as paradigmatic of the autonomy, independence, and freedom of self-employed work ("be your own boss"). To take one example: a collective of animal farmers, drawn together in opposition to the use of electronic chips on their herds, has articulated thinking which sheds light on what we have called the end of the 1980s and 90s rhetoric of the entrepreneur of the self and human capital. The small farmer, who was supposed to represent the very model of independent, autonomous, and free labor, has here been subjected to constraints that prevent him from working, if by working we mean not only performing an activity, but the possibility of understanding problems and situations and making choices. The control exercised by domestic and European administrations, which require that one scrupulously follow regulations while submitting to computer monitoring, has transformed the independent worker into a small entrepreneur, into a recipient of State aid.

Common Agricultural Policy (CAP) assistance in reality represents "debts" disbursed on the condition that "debtors" strictly adhere, throughout their operations, to what the "creditor" agencies decide: when and where to graze the animals, the number of animals per acre, etc. Everything must be reported and backed up with proof (dates, number of animals, vaccinations, diseases). Whenever a problem arises, a decision comes down from above and is uniformly applied to everyone. Sheep farmers, for example, are no longer permitted to evaluate risks and make choices based on their skills and know-how. Their actions are accounted for in advance and standardized through computer modeling, which makes them controllable. Behavior becomes automatic, includes no "value" for on-the-ground understanding, no specific assessment, but rather reproduces the assessments and evaluations codified by the administration, which the farmer has no choice but to follow.

The freedom and independence that work "in nature" was supposed to provide have made farmers dependent on institutions that regulate the production and distribution of revenues, a dependence characteristic of the indebted man.

In the controversy over "chips," our dependence is also an issue. In the West today we all receive aid, from the small business owner to the welfare user, from the farmer to the star manager, from the State worker to the subsidized artist. Whether one is actually drugged at work or not, our way of life, based on the ever-increasing importance of money, high-speed telecommunications, unlimited energy, and the omnipresent State, is itself a form of generalized assistance.[18]

Let us simply add that businesses and especially large corporations receive the most "aid" from the State.

The control of movement, behavior, and decisions is ensured by computer management tools which, through an electronic chip implanted in each animal (the same used for public transportation in Paris), enter animals and farmers into models and programs containing options and scenarios already planned out, decided on by domestic and European authorities. The microchip transforms the animal into a "flow of meat" whose number, location, health, etc., can be known in real time. The industrial just-in-time process applied to animal farming transforms the animals into "databases" and the farmers into no more than monitors of the technico-economic process they manage for the State. Farmers become "human" components of this sociotechnical and administrative process encompassing them, stripping them of any control over what they do. It is impossible to "think," to decide, and to act outside of these accounting and computer management apparatuses and their semiotics (statistics, percentages, rates, and discourses).

Farmers are deprived of the possibility of evaluating risks and taking them; they are prohibited from challenging themselves in unexpected situations, working things out, and coming up with solutions. They are restricted to following the established protocols and procedures. What puts us at risk (in the so-called "risk society"[19]) is not the complexity of the technico-socio-economic infrastructure, but the fact that the process for evaluating and deciding is detached from any kind of democratic challenge or validation and exercised instead by minority (financial, economic, political, etc.) groups, which, given their very position, are utterly "unqualified." The stakes for subjectivity, once the claim of autonomy and independence has gone, come down to an injunction to take responsibility, on an individual basis, for all the risks of the trade and the economic situation by carefully executing the authorities' directives.

The rhetoric of "human capital" and the entrepreneur of the self has faded all the more quickly since the 2007 financial crisis. This has intensified the proletarianization of social groups that had until then been made up of the self-employed as well as the proletarianization of new kinds of workers from the service and knowledge economy (following the capitalist rhetoric).

In neoliberalism, contrary to the promises of freedom and independence, the economy is administered and controlled by the State. Farmers' relationship with the administration and institutions of control is, as it is for welfare users, informed by suspicion, distrust, and hypocrisy. Like the users of social services and the beneficiaries of different social rights, farmers are potential cheats.

Privatizations have introduced management practices that concentrate and centralize evaluation in the hands of large corporations (France Télécom, Renault, etc.) and State administrations. The effects of the expropriation are literally deadly to wage-earners and users. Unemployment agencies and what is left of the Welfare State want to make the unemployed and users in general autonomous while at the same time stripping them of the possibility of making judgments for themselves. In utter contradiction to the meaning of the word "autonomy," they increase the constraints, multiply the control mechanisms, monitoring, personal counseling; they call in the unemployed and welfare recipients every month, contact them through e-mail, send them out to experience their uselessness first-hand in training courses. To make them "freer," more active and dynamic, they impose behavior, language, semiotics, and procedures. Etymologically, autonomy means to make one's own law. At the unemployment and welfare agencies, employment, competition, and the market are the law. Autonomy means being able to find one's own bearings. At the unemployment office, everything always points to employment, the market, and competition.

In the institutions of the disciplinary society (school, the army, the factory, prison), the injunction to remain passive was dominant; now, the injunction to remain "active" mobilizes subjectivities. But the activity is empty because it offers no possibility to evaluate, choose, or decide. Becoming "human capital" and being an entrepreneur of the self are the new standards of employability. The height of this deprivation came when European countries' austerity plans were put in place. Citizens were excluded from evaluation, choice, and decision-making, which was taken over by the experts (financiers, bankers, politicians, the IMF) whose actions and theories are at the root of the crisis.

Debt as Social Subjection and Machinic Subjugation

A final remark taken from Marx will allow us to examine in more detail the way in which debt/money has a "hold" on subjectivity.

> As a matter of course, the creditor possesses, besides moral guarantees, also the guarantee of legal compulsion and still other more or less real guarantees for his man.[20]

Morality, the promise, and one's word are mostly insufficient to guarantee debt repayment. To have a real "hold" on subjectivity, there must also be legal and police "machines" (Marx) as well as mnemotechnical "machines" in effect which work on and manufacture the subject (Nietzsche). Based on Deleuze and Guattari's work, it is possible to articulate the joint action of "morality" and speech on the one hand, with machines on the other. Debt/money involves subjectivity in two different but complementary ways. "Social subjection" operates molar control on the subject through the mobilization of his conscience, memory, and representations, whereas "machinic subjugation" has a molecular, infrapersonal, and pre-individual hold on subjectivity that does not pass through reflexive consciousness and its representations, nor through the "self."

Debt/money functions by constituting a legal, economic, and moral subject (creditor and debtor). It represents a powerful vector for social subjection, a mechanism for the production of individual and collective subjectivity. The Germans and the Deutsche Mark, or Americans and the dollar, are a good example of the power of this subjection (and the euro a good example of its weakness). Debt/money solicits and produces individuals' trust by appealing to their conscience, their memory, and their representations. By creating an object of identification, it powerfully contributes to their constitution as individuals/citizens of the nation.

But this *hold* on the individual would remain "discursive," ideological, "moral," were there not a form of subjectivity implicated at a molecular and pre-individual level—machinic subjugation—that did not involve consciousness, representation, or the subject. The "intersubjective" relationship founded on trust, for example, is part of the machinic function of the credit card, progressively fragmented "into sociotechnical operations and artificially recomposed as paper transactions on the monetary network."[21]

The machinic functions without the "subject." When you use an ATM, it asks you to respond to the demands of the machine, which requires you to "enter your code," "choose your amount," or "take your bills." These operations "clearly do not require acts of intellectual virtuosity—quite the opposite, one is tempted to say. What you are asked to do is to react appropriately, react quickly and without making errors, otherwise you run the risk of being momentarily excluded from the system."[22] There is no subject who *acts* here, but a "dividual" that *functions* in an "enslaved" way to the sociotechnical apparatus of the banking network. The ATM activates the "dividual" not the individual. Deleuze uses this concept to show that in machinic subjugation, "Individuals become '*dividuals*,' and masses become samples, data, markets, or '*banks*.'"[23]

The credit card is an apparatus in which the dividual functions like a cogwheel, a "human" element that conforms to the "non-human" elements of the sociotechnical machine constituted by the banking network. Social subjection mobilizes individuals, whereas machinic subjugation activates "dividuals" as "human" operators, agents, elements, or pieces of the sociotechnical machine of the debt economy. Thus, the individual "subject" writes and signs checks, he commits and gives his word, whereas the dividual's payment with a bank card

> is no more than an inscription in the hypertext of the electronic network. With the check we control our writing, since we alone can produce it, but with the bank card the only thing left is the imposition or application of a mark or trace (signature, initials, secret code, or fingerprint). The banking hypertext awaits our stimulus to carry out its transactions […]. These transactions no longer have an author, but engage in self-processing, in creating figures of meaning which

will forever remain foreign to us. The stimulus
that we provide in order to activate the system
simultaneously marks our exclusion as objective,
rational, minimally reflexive agents.[24]

The individual makes "use" of money, the dividual
is adjacent to the credit-machine, he does not act,
does not use, he functions according to the programs that use him as one of its component parts.
Debt/money asks neither trust nor consent from
the dividual. It asks only that he function correctly
according to the received instructions. And the
same is true for all the machines that we encounter
every day. Following the prescribed orders determines access to information, to money, to plane
and train tickets bought on the internet, parking
ramps, computers, bank accounts, etc.

This twofold "hold" on subjectivity, this dual
way of involving and exploiting it, is perhaps one
of the most important of Deleuze and Guattari's
contributions to our understanding of capitalism.
By considering subjection alone, current critical
theories risk withdrawing into a kind of subjective
idealism, in which there are no more machines,
machinism, sociotechnical systems, procedures, or
dividuals. Once one leaves the factory, Marx's
teachings on the "machinic" nature of capitalism
seem to be lost. In these theories, machines and
machinic subjugation disappear, whereas, in fact,

they have invaded our daily lives: we speak, see, think, and live with the assistance of all sorts of machinisms. The Foucauldian concept of governmentality also comes up short when it comes to machinic subjugation and its functioning. Government has a hold on behavior, that is, on the conduct, the actions, of individuated "subjects," but not on the machinic functioning of dividuals. Debt/money clearly represents a technique for governing behavior, but it also and above all functions as a subjugation "governing" dividuals "cybernetically" through machinic recurrence and feedback. With subjugation, "there is a process of learning the nearly automatic, procedural movements."[25]

We could make the same critique of the sociology and philosophy of the norm, of which Foucault was one of the subtlest critics. Social subjection functions according to norms, rules, and law, but subjugation, inversely, involves only protocols, techniques, procedures, instructions, and asignifying semiotics requiring reaction rather than action. Subjection implies and demands a certain self-relation, it brings into play techniques of the self. Machinic subjugation, on the other hand, dismantles the self, the subject, and the individual. The norm, the rule, and the law have a hold on the subject, but none on the dividual. Much attention has been paid to subjection. In reality, it is but one form of the production and control of subjectivity. A critique of neoliberalism must on no account neglect subjugation, since machinisms are incomparably more developed now than during the industrial age.

ANTIPRODUCTION AND ANTIDEMOCRACY

In conclusion, we must now turn our attention to the current situation. Can we still speak of a financial crisis, a nuclear crisis, a food crisis, a climate crisis? Crisis still has a positive connotation. It can refer to a situation capable of being overcome. It has long provided capitalism with the occasion for a new beginning, a New Deal, a new "pact" for new growth. Today, at least, we have the distinct impression that such is no longer the case, that we have reached a turning point, for present circumstances look less like a crisis than a catastrophe. If we understand the reasons why a New Deal is impossible today—which will allow us to better grasp the concept of "antiproduction"—we can then identify which solutions are possible and which are not for confronting today's catastrophe.

In modern-day capitalism, "production" is inseparable from "destruction," since, as Ulrich Beck suggests, terror emerges from the productive parts of society. The "considerable advances" of science simultaneously produce nuclear power capable of destroying several earth-sized planets; its "civil" uses pollute the ecosystem beyond human time and force us to live in a permanent state of exception. Industry multiplies the production of consumer goods while at the same time multiplying water, air, and soil pollution and degrading the climate. Agricultural production poisons us at the same time it provides us with food; cognitive capitalism destroys the "public" education system at every level; cultural capitalism produces historically unprecedented conformism; the image society kills imagination, and so on.

Deleuze and Guattari call this capitalist process "antiproduction" and consider it the sign of a break with capitalism as Smith, Marx, or Weber defined it. Indeed, Marx, in line with classical economists, distinguished the productive (labor employed by a capitalist) from the unproductive (domestic laborers, according to Adam Smith's example, who, although more numerous than factory workers, consumed but did not produce new wealth). This is still the point of view from which one offers critiques of "finance" for being unproductive, unlike "industry," which is considered the source of national wealth. Deleuze and Guattari argue that the productive/unproductive dichotomy no longer holds. Antiproduction establishes a new division in capitalist economic reality that goes beyond the productive/non-productive distinction because it develops within what Marx and classical political economy defined as "productive."

Antiproduction (Smith's domestic laborers, the army, the police, the "unproductive" spending of the rentier classes, etc.) does not run contrary to production, it neither restricts it nor precludes it. "This effusion from the apparatus of antiproduction is characteristic of the entire capitalist system; the capitalist effusion is that of antiproduction within production at all levels of the process."[26] The 19th century, Marx and the Marxists included, still had a "progressive" notion of capitalism. The future of humanity owed much to the development of "production" and the "producer." There was a "revolutionary" side to capitalism with regard to rent that only needed to be developed, pushed to the extreme, in order to create the conditions for another political and social system. The first half of the 20th century belied such a scenario, and following the Second World War it was obvious that a new era had begun.

Once one recognizes the presence of antiproduction within production, capitalism loses its progressive character. We can find additional confirmation of what we have argued above by considering certain of Foucault's remarks: the impossibility of reform and a new New Deal is part of antiproduction.

The permanent crisis we have been living through since the 1970s is one of the manifestations of antiproduction. With the bust of the new economy bubble, the antiproductive side came to surpass the "productive" side of capitalism. The "progressive" illusion which Silicon Valley, the dot-com economy, the new economy, etc., had implanted in people's minds, has given way to what Ulrich Beck calls the power of capitalism to "self-destruct," of which the 2007 financial collapse was but one example.[27] Antiproduction apparatuses are not only inextricable from but are above all indispensable to capitalism. Antiproduction "introduce[s] a lack where there is always too much,"[28] that is to say that growth (this "too much") is a never-fulfilled and impossible promise of happiness, since antiproduction produces a lack in whatever level of wealth a nation achieves.

Capitalism is not only a system that continuously expands its limits, it is also an apparatus that infinitely reproduces, independently of the level of wealth achieved, conditions of exploitation and domination, that is, conditions of "lack." The "weak" growth of the last thirty years has doubled the GDP of Western countries, while deepening social, economic, and political inequality. Modern-day antiproduction (the antiproduction of the knowledge society, cultural capitalism, cognitive capitalism) has not only worsened the economic conditions of the vast majority of the population, it is also a subjective catastrophe. As *Anti-Oedipus* humorously puts it, antiproduction

> doubles the capital and the flow of knowledge with a capital and an equivalent flow of *stupidity* that [...] ensures the integration of groups and individuals into the system. Not only lack amid overabundance, but stupidity in the midst of knowledge and science [...].[29]

One need only add the art, culture, and communication colonized by the culture industry as sites and vectors of "stupidity." Cognitive and cultural capitalism does not endow subjectivity with "knowledge" but with stupidity, even when qualified or overqualified (BA, MBA, PhD).

> Here Andre Gorz's double portrait of the "scientific and technical worker" takes on its full meaning. Although he has mastered a flow of knowledge, information, and training, he is so absorbed in capital that the reflux of organized, axiomatized stupidity coincides with him, so that, when he goes home in the evening, he rediscovers his little desiring-machines by tinkering with a television set—O despair. Of course the scientist as such has no revolutionary potential;

he is the first integrated agent of integration, a refuge for bad conscience, and the *forced* destroyer of his own creativity.[30]

Fifteen years later, the sociology of the "risk society" would come up with a watered-down theory of antiproduction in which it completely loses its political connotations and political force. Ulrich Beck, the pope of the risk society, does this in two ways. First, he recognizes the "power of self-destruction of capitalism triumphant." The "social production of wealth" is now inseparable from "the social production of risks." The old politics for redistributing the "goods" of the industrial society (income, labor, social welfare) has combined with a politics for distributing "ills" (ecological risks and dangers). "Those who put the nation at risk today are those responsible for law, order, rationality, and democracy itself."[31] Furthermore, not only does he clear those "responsible" of all responsibility, he makes antiproduction humanity's only hope for salvation. In the case of nuclear power, for example, the practices and forms of mobilization of the antinuclear movement, that is, the forms of collective thought and action, could never create, according to him, the conditions necessary for forcing a reversal on energy policies. "In the last analysis, if there is a challenge to nuclear energy, it should be sought less among the protesters blocking the transportation of fuel. The mainspring of opposition to nuclear energy lies in the nuclear industry itself,"[32] since the industry and institutions are supposed to have acquired a capacity to identify the problems and reflect on them which allows them to adjust, correct, adapt, and improve their activities under the influence of a citizenry itself enlightened by such self-awareness. The mountain of the "second modernity" has engendered a molehill of power that has morphed into a counter-power, into self-awareness and a capacity of companies like Tepco, which managed the Fukushima nuclear plant, to reflect on their strategy, discuss it, and modify it. By the same logic, the "mainspring of opposition" to debt politics is none other than the power bloc that led to the financial catastrophe in the first place. We are going to be waiting a long a time for this supposed self-awareness of the second modernity. Indeed, now that losses have been nationalized, the "awareness" that banks, investors, and insurance companies have adopted is the following: "Everything must go on just as it did before!"

Contrary to the consensual theory of the "risk society," which is part of modern-day capitalist rhetoric, the only way to stop and turn back, not the "risks" of financialization, but the destructive power of debt (the antiproduction of contemporary capitalism now manifest in the politics of indebtedness), lies in the capacity of debtors to think and act collectively. Exactly as in industrial societies, "awareness" must be imposed on the institutions and structures of government through a struggle that divides society, that breaks the consensus. The exact same thing can be said about nuclear policies. Change depends solely on the strength of the antinuclear movement, and certainly not on the self-awareness of the nuclear industry and the authorities. Only just recently in Italy and Germany, the abandonment of nuclear power was *imposed* on industry and government. The only self-awareness the nuclear industry and the financial power bloc are capable of is the following: how do we keep going until catastrophe hits? "Everything must go on just as it did before": that is Benjamin's very definition of catastrophe.

Debt functions in such a way as to sweep aside the politics of "panels" of citizens, experts and counter-experts, politicians, businesspeople, etc. It completely eliminates the consensual democracy of a "second democracy" à la Beck, since the current process is utterly different.

The debt economy is characterized not only by antiproduction but also by what we might call antidemocracy. If we use the categories of political regimes established by the "Greeks," we can easily see that credit is not the site of "public evaluation" in which the power of the people (democracy) is exercised. Quite the opposite, for forty years of neoliberal policies have undermined already weak representative institutions and the crisis has strengthened all the political systems the Greeks considered opposed to democracy. Choices and decisions concerning whole peoples have been made by an oligarchy, a plutocracy, and an aristocracy (the power of the "best," quite well-represented by ratings agencies, which are the best experts due solely to their sensitivity to the interests of creditors). Taken together, the three antidemocratic regimes produce corruption rather than growth. In certain European countries (Italy, Greece, Spain, the UK), such is more obviously the case than elsewhere, and yet it concerns us all. Corruption, hypocrisy, and distrust are not the phenomena of a *mal governo*, but, as Marx reminds us, a structural condition of the politics of debt and credit. With the threat of national defaults, therefore, the oldest counter-revolutionary project, the Trilateral Commission (1973) is being fulfilled: to govern the economy through drastic limits to democracy and a no less drastic drop in the expectations of the governed.

In early July 2011, the Italian government presented an austerity plan with the goal of 87.7 billion euros in savings by 2014. In addition to being as unfair as those adopted by other European governments, the plan contained some ambiguity as to the content and timeline of its implementation. It took only two days of speculation on Italian sovereign debt to speed up the process. A day after a massive selloff of State securities by investors, the majority and the opposition, under "market" pressure, rushed to agree on the plan. National governments and parliaments are mere executors of the decisions and timelines decided outside what one still calls national "sovereignty."

The difficulty for liberalism is not, as Foucault believed, that of "governing as little as possible," but rather, pushed by the contradictions it engenders and exacerbates, that of ruling and controlling as much as possible with "as little democracy as possible." In liberalism, there is no competition; there is instead an unprecedented monopoly on and centralization of power and money. In forty years, neoliberalism has become an economy that, given what has happened with sovereign debt, can only be defined as an "extortion economy." In the same vein, the management of "human resources" in businesses and social services has been carried out under threats of unemployment and relocation. The same political extortion constantly looms over political conflicts regarding retirement and social services. It is thus completely logical that a criminal economy has developed in parallel with liberalism and become at once a structural phenomenon and linchpin. Extortion is the mode of "democratic" government to which neoliberalism leads.

Conclusion

An essential question thus arises: Under what conditions can we revive a class struggle that capitalism has completely shifted to the very "abstract" and "deterritorialized" ground of debt?

Marx said that crises managed to impress on the hackneyed thinking of capitalists certain things they otherwise would never have accepted. Here, the "thinking" to impress is that of leaders and intellectuals on the political and labor-union left, since debt really ought to immediately dispel their illusions. As a battleground, debt cuts across every domain: States and national space, the economic, the political, and the social, figures of exploitation and domination. We must rise to this level of abstraction and deterritorialization if we want to avoid being swept away or crushed by the Great Creditor.

The political space in which to begin the fight cannot, under any circumstances, be that of the nation State. Debt ignores boundaries and nationalities; at the level of the world-economy, it knows only creditors and debtors. For the same reasons, it forces us to shift our perspective from labor and employment in order to conceive a politics at the level of Capital as "Universal Creditor." Debt surpasses the divisions between employment and unemployment, working and non-working, productive and assisted, precarious and non-precarious, divisions on which the left has based its categories of thought and action.

The figure of "indebted man" cuts across the whole of society and calls for new solidarities and new cooperation. We must also take into account how it pervades "nature and culture," since neoliberalism has run up our debt to the planet as well as to ourselves as living beings.

One of the essential conditions for advancing the class struggle is the reinvention of "democracy" as it traverses and reconfigures what even very sophisticated political theories continue to conceive of separately—the political, the social, and the economic—since debt has already united them within a single apparatus. The debt economy appears to fully realize the mode of government suggested by Foucault. To be effective, it must control the social sphere and the population—the latter transformed into an indebted population. Such is the essential condition for governing the heterogeneity of politics and the economy, but within an authoritarian—and no longer "liberal" —regime. Because politics cannot be reduced to power, because politics is not simply the positive side of a negative politics of debt, because politics cannot be isolated from the economy (of debt), political action within capitalism has never emerged except from within and against the politics of Capital. How is one to invent the reasons for a "wrong" and the conditions for "dispute" without starting from the relations of current exploitation and domination? The negative that debt institutes informs the historical conditions from which struggle turns away to invent new forms of subjectivation and new possibilities of life. Still, these conditions are indeed, at each instance, historical, unique, and specific. And today they come together in debt.

The most urgent task consists in imagining and experimenting with forms of struggle which are as effective at bringing things to a halt as strikes were in industrial society. The level of deterritorialization of capitalist control demands it. The stale thinking of capitalists and politicians only register the language of crisis and combat.

If we have here laid out a theoretical and political framework centered on the debt economy, it has not been so much to provide a new general and global theory of neoliberalism as to offer a transversal point of view from which struggles might begin.

The fight against the debt economy and above all against its "morality" of guilt, which, in the end, is a morality of fear, also requires a specific kind of subjective conversion. Nietzsche again offers us some idea: "atheism might release humanity from this whole feeling of being indebted towards its beginnings, its *causa prima*. Atheism and a sort of *second innocence* belong together."[1]

The resumption of the class struggle in the right place, that is, where it is the most effective, must recapture this "second innocence" with respect to debt. A second innocence no longer toward divine debt, but toward mundane debt, the debt that weighs in our wallets and forms and formats our subjectivities. This not only means annulling debts or calling for default, even if that too would be quite useful, but leaving behind debt morality and the discourse in which it holds us hostage.

We have lost a lot of time, and lost a lot, period, by trying to clear our debts. In doing so, we are already guilty! We must recapture this second innocence, rid ourselves of guilt, of everything owed, of all bad conscience, and not repay a cent. We must fight for the cancellation of debt, for debt, one will recall, is not an economic problem but an apparatus of power designed not only to impoverish us, but to bring about catastrophe.

The financial catastrophe is far from over, since no regulation of finance is possible. Its regulation would mark the end of neoliberalism. Moreover, the oligarchies, plutocracies, and "aristocracies" in power have no alternative political program. What the IMF, Europe, and the European Central Bank demand, themselves blackmailed by the "markets," are still, as always, neoliberal remedies that only make the situation worse. With the second Greek austerity plan—and even if the ratings agencies' bets on a partial Greek default pay off—the consequences for the European people will remain the same. They will be bled to death regardless. The threat of debt looms over all Europeans like inevitable fate. There is only one possibility: reimburse the Great Creditor! The sole institutions that have made out well in the latest financial collapse are the banks, which continue to make profits and hand out bonuses thanks to the nationalization of their losses. But the problem has only been shifted elsewhere. Unless we come up with a debt—no longer sovereign, but cosmic—in such a way as to create and exploit an extraterrestrial financial bubble, it is impossible to see how we can make it out of this catastrophe while continuing to apply and impose the very principles that caused it. Capitalism always functions in this way: a feverish and hypermodern deterritorialization, which expands its frontiers forever further, along with a racist, nationalist, machinist, patriarchal, and authoritarian reterritorialization that makes life wretched—"living and dying like pigs," as Gilles Châtelet puts it, with the due respect we owe pigs—a way of life that the Italy of Berlusconi put on display with peerless vulgarity.

In an interview on Greek television in 1992, Félix Guattari, sardonic and provocative, disclosed the hidden objectives of finance that today weigh bitterly on "small" European States:

> Greece is the bad sheep of Europe. That's its virtue. Good thing there are black sheep like Greece to mix things up, to refuse a certain Germano-French standardization, etc. So, continue being black sheep and we'll get along just fine…

— Naples, July 15, 2011

DEBT AND AUSTERITY: THE GERMAN MODEL OF PRECARIOUS FULL-EMPLOYMENT

[T]he faction of the bourgeoisie that ruled and legislated through the Chambers had a direct interest in the indebtedness of the state. The state deficit was really the main object of its speculation and the chief source of its enrichment. At the end of each year a new deficit. After the lapse of four or five years a new loan. And every new loan offered new opportunities to the finance aristocracy for defrauding the state, which was kept artificially on the verge of bankruptcy—it had to negotiate with the bankers under the most unfavorable conditions. Each new loan gave a further opportunity, that of plundering the public which invested its capital in state bonds...
—Karl Marx, *The Class Struggles in France*[1]

The way out of the crisis can only be found outside the programs proposed by the IMF. Again and again this institution puts forward the same kind of fiscal adjustments, which consist in cutting the money we give to citizens—wages, pensions, public assistance in addition to public work projects that create jobs—in order to use the money saved to pay creditors. It's nonsense. After four years of crisis, we can't keep on taking money from the same people. Now, this is exactly what they want to do to Greece! Cut everything in order to give it to the banks. The IMF has been transformed into an institution designed to protect financial interests alone. When you're in dire straits, as Argentina was in 2001, you have to be able to completely change the way you think about things.

—Roberto Lavagna, Former Argentine Minister of
    Economy and Production, 2002 to 2005

Fewer than twenty years after the "decisive victory over communism" and just fifteen years since "the end of history," capitalism has reached an historical dead end. Since 2007, it has survived solely through injections of astronomical sums of public money. Yet despite this, it is on its last legs. At best, it reproduces itself, but only by frantically doing away with what remains of the social gains of the last two centuries.

Since the "sovereign debt crises," it has made a comic spectacle of how it functions. The "rational" economic norms which the "markets," ratings agencies, and experts have imposed on State governments in order for them to recover from the public debt crisis are the same as those that caused both the private and public debt crises. Banks, pension funds, and institutional investors require states to put their public balance sheets in order while still holding billions in junk securities, the result of policies designed to replace wages and income with credit. After giving AAA ratings to securities which are worthless today (in a bank study of 2,679 of 17,000 mortgage-backed securities rated by S&P, 99% of the sample were given a AAA rating at issue, whereas 90% are now rated "non-investment grade"), ratings agencies claim, despite evidence to the contrary, that their economic measures are still exact and their ratings accurate. The experts (economics professors, consultants, bankers, civil servants, etc.), whose blindness to the destruction that market self-regulation and competition have wrought on society and the planet—a blindness directly proportional to their intellectual servility—have been catapulted into "technocratic" governments which can only recall the "bourgeois business committee." Yet these represent less "technocratic governments" than new authoritarian and repressive "government techniques" which break with classical "liberalism" itself.

But the most ludicrous actor in all this is perhaps the media. The "information" provided by news programs and talk shows tells us that "the crisis is your fault, because you're retiring too early, seeking too much medical care, aren't sufficiently flexible, consume too much in public services. That is, you're guilty of living beyond your means."

Advertising, on the other hand, with its continual interruptions of the guilt-inducing speeches of economists, journalists, and politicians, proclaims exactly the opposite. "You're absolutely innocent, you have no responsibilities! Neither errors nor guilt stain your soul. You deserve everything without exception, for you've earned the paradise of our merchandise. It is even your duty to consume compulsively."

The "orders" and injunctions conveyed by the signifying semiotics of guilt and the iconic and symbolic semiotics of innocence are now in open conflict. The ascetic ethic of work and debt and the hedonistic ethic of mass consumption can no longer be reconciled but overtly contradict each other.

Instead of offering a way out of the crisis, all this confusion resembles a vicious circle in which capitalism is now stuck. Since our elites never see beyond their own pocket books, one must expect the worst. The ferocity with which governments, technocratic or not, have pursued debt reimbursement and defended private property continues unabated (according to the *New York Times*, bank representatives and Greek debt holders have sought recourse to the European Court of Human Rights because Greece is supposed to have violated their fundamental rights, for "property rights are human rights"). But the recession and depression (Greece) are minor evils compared to the possibility of breaking the promise of paying the debt. In a recent interview, the ECB president proposed, with Thatcherian cynicism, the same recipes that led to the crisis to begin with and will surely make it worse: lower taxes to fatten the rich and reductions in social spending to impoverish the poor.

Politicians have been reduced to the accountants and "proxies" (Marx) of capital. French President Nicolas Sarkozy has recommended that money to pay "interest on Greek debt be deposited in a blocked account, which would thereby guarantee that the debts of our Greek friends are paid." "Partial" to the idea, German Chancellor Angela Merkel has agreed that it would "ensure that the money would be available over the long term."

If there is a constant of capitalism, it is indeed that of the state of war to which liberalism almost "automatically" leads. Inter-capitalist war now looks less severe than that which each national capitalism wages against its own domestic enemies. Although in disagreement as to how to divide the spoils of worldwide exploitation, the different capitalisms agree on how to intensify the war waged within each State. To overcome the crisis, the time has therefore come for structural "reforms." Does this mean regulating finance? Redistributing wealth? Reducing inequalities, precarity, or unemployment? The end of shameful Welfare State "assistance" and tax breaks to business and the rich? No, the sole "structural reforms" envisioned and implemented are the following: the restructuring of the labor market coupled with drops in wages and drastic cuts in public spending beginning, as usual, with unemployment insurance. The model for this is Germany. In a recent television performance, Sarkozy managed to mention the German example nine times, while Mario Monti's technocratic government remains equally under the charm of the new "iron lady" from whom both receive their "advice" (read: orders) directly.

The German Model

For the last ten years Germany has pursued policies of labor market flexibilization and precarization as well as stark cuts in the Welfare State. In the European Parliament, Daniel Cohn-Bendit asked Angela Merkel, "How is it possible that a rich country like Germany has 20% of its population living in poverty?"[2] Is the ex-*soixante-huitard* [a participant in the demonstrations of May '68] naïve or a pitiable amnesiac? More likely, a hypocritical cynic, since it was in fact former Chancellor Schröder's "Red-Green" government that between 2000 and 2005 introduced the bulk of the laws at the origin of the current situation, a situation in which "precarious full-employment" has transformed the unemployed and "inactive" into an awesome mass of "poor workers." Just a little history and a handful of data are needed to uncover the misery of the German model, which the Troika (Europe, the IMF, and the ECB) is now imposing on every European country.

Rallying to the slogan "Fördern und Fordern" (literally, supporting and requiring—or carrot and stick), between 1999 and 2005 the Red-Green government pushed through four major reforms of unemployment insurance and the labor market, one more catastrophic than the next (the Hartz reforms I-IV).

In January 2003, Hartz II introduced "mini-job" contracts, which created a kind of legalized under-the-table work (exempting employers from payroll taxes and providing employees with neither unemployment insurance nor pension contributions). It also established so-called "midi-job" contracts (for earnings of 400 to 800 euros per month), encouraging people to become the "entrepreneurs" of their own misery.

In January 2004, the Hartz III reform restructured national and federal employment agencies with a view to increasing the control and monitoring of poor workers' lives and behavior. Once the measures for governing poor workers were set, the Red-Green government approved a staggering series of laws designed to "produce" such workers.

Taking effect on January 1, 2005, Hartz IV provided for the following:

• A reduction in the duration of compensation from three years to a maximum of one; a restriction on access to compensation, requiring the unemployed to accept any job offered. The right to unemployment insurance now depends on one's having been employed for twelve months over the two years preceding the loss of work. After a year of unemployment benefits, the unemployed person receives welfare assistance of 359 euros, since raised to 374 euros. A report issued by the federal employment agency has shown that one out of four workers who lose their job receives welfare assistance (Arbeitslosengeld II, or ALG II) without ever receiving unemployment benefits (ALG I). This has to do with the nature of the job the worker has lost, in these cases precarious or poorly paid.

• A reduction in benefits paid to the long-term unemployed who refuse to accept work below their qualifications.

• The unemployed must accept positions with wages of one euro per hour (added to the unemployment benefits they receive).

• A possible reduction in benefits to the unemployed holding savings and, consequently, the government's right to access the bank accounts of those drawing benefits. In addition, the government may dictate the acceptable size of a beneficiary's residence and, consequently, may also demand that the beneficiary change residence.

It is estimated that up to 6.6 million people—among whom 1.7 million children—receive Hartz IV welfare benefits. 4.9 million adults are in reality poor workers employed less than 15 hours per week. In May 2011, the official statistics showed upwards of five million mini-jobs, an increase of 47.7%, exceeded only by the boom in intermittent work (+134%). These types of jobs are also very common among retirees, 660,000 of whom supplement their pensions with a mini-job.[3] A large portion of the population, 21.7%, was employed part-time in 2010. The German Federal Statistics Office (Destatis) has measured the rise in precarity in its various forms: between 1999 and 2009, all atypical kinds of work increased by at least 20%.[4] The most affected are single-parent families (mostly women) and seniors. In conditions of precarious full-employment, the official unemployment rate, hailed as proof of the "German economic miracle," doesn't amount to much.

The growing army of poor workers is not only composed of the precarious but also of workers under short-term contracts. In August 2010, a report by the Institute for Work, Skills and

Training at the University of Duisburg-Essen revealed that more than 6.55 million Germans gross less than 10 euros an hour, that is, an increase of 2.26 million over ten years. The numbers are mostly composed of the former unemployed whom the Hartz system has managed to "put to work": those under 25 years old, foreigners, and women (69% of the total). Moreover, 2 million workers earn less than 6 euros an hour; in the former East Germany, many live on less than 4 euros, in other words, less than 720 euros per month working full-time. The result? Poor workers represent nearly 20% of all German workers.

During the financial crisis, the government massively resorted to partial unemployment, allowing businesses to pay workers just 60% of their normal salary and to pay only half the normal payroll taxes. Another result of the Schröder watershed: wages have dropped by 5% of GDP in Germany since 2002.

The changes the "Red-Greens" have introduced are, moreover, qualitative. After years of a chaotic and brutal spread of precarity as well as increasing numbers of underemployed and underpaid, it was time to regulate and rationalize poverty and precarity by creating a "real" and "coherent" labor market of "beggars." Such a market aims to force flexibility and economic reason even on those with the best jobs. The whole of the working population—precarious, poor, and well-qualified —has been made to "float," compelled to adapt to permanent flexibilization. The different segments of the "labor force" are now but adjustment variables of economic conditions.

The "Red-Green" program was aptly named "Agenda 2010,"[5] for ten years after the first Hartz law the results have been literally fatal. The life expectancy of the poorest—those who earn only three-fourths the average income—has been consistently falling in Germany. For low-income earners, it has dropped from 77.5 years old in 2001 to 75.6 in 2011 according to official numbers. In the former East Germany things are even worse: life expectancy has gone from 77.9 to 74.1.

Germany has led European countries in following the United States down the path of neoliberalism. Just another twenty years' effort to "save the retirement system" and death will finally coincide with the retirement age. The domestic war has also had its targeted "surgical strikes." All things being equal, in the former East Germany life expectancy will shortly drop to 66 years old, only a year before the retirement age of 67. "Mors tua, vita mea!" No matter! The economy is healthy, "agencies" award it good ratings, creditors grow fat, and life expectancy among the richest of the population continues to climb.

Therefore, a word or two must be said about Peter Hartz, whose ideas were behind the laws on unemployment insurance and public assistance. The two-year suspended sentence and 576,000 euro fine he received perfectly illustrate the "corruption" consubstantial with the neoliberal model. Former human resources chief at Volkswagen and great moralizer of the "Anspruchdenker"—the "profiteers of the system"—Peter Hartz finally admitted to funneling cash to Klaus Volkert, union leader at IG Metall and former president of the labor-management committee at the car manufacturer, in order to pay for prostitutes and extravagant trips. As for Klaus Volkert, he was brought to court for encouraging fraud with his alleged accomplice, former personnel director Klaus-Joachim Gebauer.

Making poverty and precarization a strategic variable of labor market flexibility is what is now happening in Italy, Portugal, Greece, Spain,[6] the UK, and Ireland—each blackmailed with the threat of exorbitant debt. France has followed suit since Sarkozy came to power, even if the results have been less spectacular than in Germany. Thanks once again to a man of the center-left, Martin Hirsch, hired on by the conservative French president in his "move to the left," France has endeavored to transform public assistance (the RMI, Revenu minimum d'insertion, of 454 euros per month per person) into a weapon for producing poor workers (now the RSA, Revenu de solidarité active).[7] Through techniques for governing the poor, power and control apparatuses are first tested in order to then expand them to the whole of society, a project which neither the left nor the unions seem to find the least bit troubling.

The RSA goes beyond the old Fordist dualisms (unemployment/employment, wages/income, the right to work/the right to social services, law/contract) in order to intertwine and combine them in the figure of the poor worker. It permanently institutes a worker/beneficiary status, which allows one to draw wages for work and welfare income at the same time. This blurring of "wage-earning" and "beneficiary" status, of employment, unemployment, and social assistance, the right to work and the right to public services, provides the basis for the creation of a second labor market, whose norm is underemployment and underpaid work. The RSA thus marks the official abandonment of the goal of full-employment as it implements a policy of "full activity" conceived as work for everyone regardless of the duration and type.[8]

Using the blackmail of debt, the State seeks to complete the move begun in the 1980s from welfare (rights and social services) to workfare (the subordination of social policies to the availability and flexibility of precarious full-employment). The authoritarian turn of neoliberalism is in the process of doing away with the "European social model," for, as Mario Draghi has said, it is no longer acceptable to "pay people who don't work."

With each new economic-political phase, we find the State and its administration taking the lead in the process. Just as it facilitated and encouraged the neoliberal lending policies of the 1980s and 1990s, the State has ensured they continue under new authoritarian and repressive forms of debt reimbursement and the figure of the indebted man. Yet another leftist illusion has thus fallen, that of opposing the logic of private property with the logic of a state-ensured "public" domain. The political is not autonomous nor is the State neutral. Its administration decisively *acts on* the economy, "society," and subjectivities as the restructuring of the labor market demonstrates in a paradigmatic way.

A Financial Crisis or a Crisis of Capitalism?

It is less important to show the omnipotence of capitalism than to recognize its weaknesses over the medium and long term. While the structural counter-reforms dramatically affect a large portion of the population, they fail to point a way out of the crisis. The experts, the markets, the ratings agencies, and politicians don't know where to go or how to go about it, and behind the blackmail of deficits, they do no more than extend neoliberal policies of production and intensify the class differences that are the true source of the crisis.

The capitalist machine has gone off the rails, not for want of regulation nor because of its so-called excesses or the greed of financiers (again, illusions of the regulating "left"!), etc. While true, these fail to capture the nature of the current crisis, which began prior to the collapse of finance. Indeed, the latter is the consequence of the failure of the neoliberal program (which has made business the model for all social relations) and of the resistance mounted by the subjective figure it has aimed to promote (human capital or the entrepreneur of the self). Even passive, such resistance has transformed credit into debt by obstructing the neoliberal program. If credit and money manifest their common nature as "debt," it is because accumulation has been blocked and thus can no longer ensure new profits and produce new forms of subjection and not the other way around.

Between 2001 and 2004, 10% GDP growth in the US was possible only because measures designed to boost economic activity injected 15.5 points of GDP into the economy: lower taxes worth 2.5 GDP points, with a rise in real estate loans from 450 to 960 billion dollars (1.3 trillion just before the 2007 crisis) and an increase in public spending of 500 billion dollars.

In Germany at the turn of the century the same thing occurred. German GDP growth between 2000 and 2006 was 354 billion euros. But if we compare the debt figures over the same period (342 billion), it is easy to see that the actual result was "zero growth."

But Japan was the first to achieve "zero growth," followed by recession, from the time the real estate bubble burst in the 1990s (with debt, used to bail out the banking system, exploding in its turn). The Japanese experience reveals better than in other countries the nature of the current crisis. The reasons for the impasse of the neoliberal model must be sought not only in economic contradictions, although quite real, but also and above all in what Félix Guattari called the "crisis of the production of subjectivity."

The Japanese miracle, which succeeded in creating a collective workforce and a social force "thoroughly integrated with machinism" (Guattari), now appears to be running out of steam, for Japan, like all developed countries, finds itself trapped in debt and its modes of subjectivation. The "Fordist" subjective model (lifetime employment, a period dedicated solely to work, the role of the family and its patriarchal division of roles, etc.) no longer holds and no one knows with what it should be replaced.

The debt crisis has not revealed the folly of speculation, but rather the attempt to keep a moribund capitalism alive. The German "economic miracle" is a *regressive* and *authoritarian* response to the impasses already manifest before 2007. This is why Germany and Europe have been so harsh and inflexible with Greece. Not only because "I want my money back" (creditors' money), but also and above all because the financial crisis has ushered in a new political phase in which capital can no longer count on the "promise of future wealth" for everyone as in the 1980s. The illusions of the "freedom" and "independence" of human capital, or those of the information society and cognitive capitalism, are no longer available. To speak like Marx, it can only extend and expand "absolute surplus value," that is, prolong labor time, increase unpaid work, impose cuts in wages and all public services, lower living conditions, multiply precarious work, diminish life expectancy, etc. Austerity, the demand for sacrifices, and the creation of the subjective figure of the debtor do not constitute a rough stretch as we advance toward "new growth," but techniques of power whose authoritarianism, now devoid of anything "liberal," can alone guarantee the reproduction of power relations. Governing precarious full-employment and extorting debt payments have required the inclusion of large portions of the far-right program in the democratic political system; indeed, since at least the 1980s, the latter has functioned according to something other than representation.

Since 2007, passive resistance, having forgone the neoliberal program, has in various ways begun and now represents the only hope for escaping the "government techniques" of the "technocratic governments" of debt. Seeing the disasters of the austerity plans visited on Greece, we must each repeat to ourselves, one way or another, "de te fabula narratur"! (For this story does indeed apply to you.)

—March 5, 2012

Notes

1. Understanding Debt as the Basis of Social Life

1. *Union nationale interprofessionnelle pour l'emploi dans l'industrie et le commerce* (National Interprofessional Union for Employment in Industry and Trade).

2. Repayment on capital, which is part of debt service, represents around 80 billion euros for France, that is, the amount of all other direct tax receipts (corporate taxes, etc.). The State's total debt service represents 118 billion euros, the entirety of its direct tax resources, or nearly its total take from the VAT (around 130 billion euros).

3. E. M. Mouhoud and D. Plihon, *Le Savoir et la finance* (Knowledge and Finance) (Paris: La Découverte, 2009), 124.

4. "Compared to consumer credit, payment by credit card is a veritable qualitative bond. Whereas the latter used to be made only upon explicit request, the card system automates credit; the reversal of initiative here is exemplary, for with credit cards the credit relationship is always already in place—now one need only use the card to activate it [...]. The card payment system institutes a permanent debt structure. We are permanent debtors to some commercial or banking entity; we permanently receive an advance on income." A. J. Haesler, Sociologie de l'argent et post-modernité (*Sociology of Money and Postmodernity*) (Geneva: Droz, 1995), 282.

5. G. Ardant, *Histoire financière de l'antiquité à nos jours* (A History of Finance from Antiquity to Today) (Paris: Gallimard, 1976), 320.

6. Ibid., 442.

7. K. Marx, *Capital*, vol. 3, trans. David Fernbach (New York: Penguin Classics, 1991), 567.

8. C. Marazzi, *The Violence of Financial Capitalism, new edition* (Semiotext(e), 2011), 27–28 (translation modified).

9. Securitization is the financial practice of transferring financial assets such as debt (for example, outstanding loans or credit card receivables) to investors by transforming that debt via an ad hoc company into financial securities issued on capital markets. In the language of the market, a security designates an asset, a stock, a loan, etc. For example, one says that a bank is "securitizing" when it converts an asset into a security it lists on the market.

10. Businesses do not turn to financial markets to finance their investments but prefer to self-finance. All large companies listed on the stock market self-finance; they use equity capital up to 90% of their financing needs. They turn to financial markets to increase their "rent" share, the share not generated from within the company.

11. G. Duménil and D. Lévy, "La finance capitaliste: rapports de production et rapports de classe" (Capitalist Finance: Production Relations and Class Relations), in *La Finance capitaliste* (Paris: PUF, 2006), 167.

12. M. Anglietta and A. Orléan, *La monnaie entre violence et confiance* (Money: between Violence and Trust) (Paris: Odile Jacob, 2002), 244.

13. D. Kessler, "L'avenir de la protection sociale" (The Future of Social Protections), *Commentaire*, no. 87 (Autumn, 1999): 625.

14. Ibid., 622.

15. M. Aglietta and A. Orléan, op. cit., 182.

16. Ibid., 248.

17. In the US, 80% of law students obtain their degree $77,000 in debt, on average, if they attended a private university and $50,000 in debt if they attended a public one. The average debt of students receiving a degree in medicine is, according to a study of the Association of American Colleges, $140,000. A female student having just finished her law degree confessed to an Italian newspaper, "I don't think I will be able to pay back the debts I owe for my education. Sometimes I think that when I die I will still have monthly payments to make for university. I currently have a repayment plan spread over 27 and a half years, but that is too ambitious since the interest is variable and I am only able to pay it back at a certain rate. I am very careful with my spending; I note every expense, from coffee to a bus ticket […]. Everything has to be planned […]. The thing that worries me the most is that I am incapable of saving, and my debt is always there looming over me." *Repubblica* (August 4, 2008).

18. G. Deleuze, *Nietzsche and Philosophy*, trans. Hugh Tomlinson (New York: Continuum, 2002), 155. As early as this book from 1963 Deleuze was dealing with debt and its effects on subjectivity.

19. G. Deleuze, *Negotiations, 1972–1990*, trans. Martin Joughin (New York: Columbia University Press, 1995), 152.

2. The Genealogy of Debt and the Debtor

1. F. Nietzsche, *On the Genealogy of Morality and Other Writings*, trans. Carol Diethe (Cambridge: Cambridge University Press, 2006), 24.

2. Ibid., 45.

3. G. Deleuze and F. Guattari, *Anti-Oedipus*, trans. Robert Hurley (Minneapolis: University of Minnesota Press, 1983), 190.

4. F. Nietzsche, *On the Genealogy of Morality*, op. cit., 38.

5. Ibid., 40.

6. Ibid., 36.

7. Ibid.

8. Ibid., 40–41.

9. Ibid., 58.

10. G. Deleuze and F. Guattari, *Anti-Oedipus*, op cit., 190, and F. Nietzsche, *On the Genealogy of Morality*, op. cit., 36.

11. Ibid., 36.

12. J. Le Goff, *Your Money or Your Life*, trans. Patricia Ranum (New York: Zone Books, 2001), 39.

13. Ibid., 40–41.

14. K. Marx, "Comments on James Mill—Éléments d'économie politique Translated by J. T. Parisot—Paris, 1823," in *Karl Marx, Frederick Engels: Collected Works, vol. 3, Marx and Engels: 1843–1844*, trans. Jack Cohen (New York: International Publishers, 2005), 211–228. (All subsequent quotations in this section are taken from this text.)

15. K. Marx, *Capital*, vol. 3, op. cit., 528.

16. Ibid., 490.

17. Ibid., 490–491.

18. Ibid., 491.

19. Ibid., 570.

20. V. I. Lenin, "Imperialism, the Highest Stage of Capitalism," *Essential Works of Lenin* (New York: Bantam Books, 1966), 193.

21. All of the authors mentioned in what follows—James, Nietzsche, Pascal, and Deleuze—describe what the latter terms a substitution of the model of faith for one of knowledge, which provides another serious reason to suspect the relevance of the paradigm offered by "cognitive capitalism." Even science, the productive force par excellence of the paradigm, requires something other than knowledge to exist: "a philosophy, a 'faith' always has to be there first, for knowledge to win from it a direction, a meaning, a limit, a method, a *right* to exist. [...] Our faith in science is still based on a *metaphysical faith*," Nietzsche, op. cit., 112. It is impossible to conceive modern-day "production" as a "production of knowledge by means of knowledge." The production of something new, whether economic, political, or subjective, requires something other than "knowledge."

22. W. James, *Writings 1878–1899* (New York: Library of America, 1992), 518, 1049.

23. Ibid., 472–473, 472, 531.

24. Ibid., 458, 529.

25. W. Benjamin, "Experience and Poverty," and "The Destructive Character," *Selected Writings, Vol. 2, part 2, 1931–1934*, trans. Rodney Livingstone (Cambridge: Harvard University Press, 2005), 732, 542.

26. Benjamin's "barbarian" resembles in significant ways James's "tough-minded," pluralists who are able to adapt to an instable and uncertain world, a truth in the process of becoming, a world in which actualities are among "a wider sea of possibilities." The "tender-minded" are "rationalists" who redeem the uncertain world by transforming it into "another world," "a better world," in which particular things form an absolute unity that encompasses them

and gives them stability and meaning. W. James, *Pragmatism and Other Writings* (New York: Penguin, 2000), 11.

27. W. James, *Writings 1878–1899*, op. cit., 1050, 650.

28. James provides an example of the way in which subjective elements come to determine the power to act as well as events in the world. He uses a concrete example, a dangerous leap during a mountain hike: "It is only by risking our persons from one hour to another that we live at all. And often enough our faith before-hand in an uncertified result *is the only thing that makes the result come true.* Suppose, for instance, that you are climbing a mountain, and have worked yourself into a position from which the only escape is by a terrible leap. Have faith that you can success-fully make it, and your feet are nerved to its accomplishment. But mistrust yourself [...] and you will hesitate so long that, at last, all unstrung and trembling, and launching yourself in a moment of despair, you roll in the abyss. In such a case [...], the part of wisdom as well as of courage is to *believe what is in the line of your needs,* for only by such belief is the need fulfilled. Refuse to believe, and you shall indeed be right, for you shall irretriev-ably perish. But believe, and again you shall be right, for you shall save yourself," ibid., 500. This in no way means that will equals power, since subjectivity does no more than add some-thing to the world: the interpretation of signs that affect it. "Suppose that in looking at the world and seeing how full it is of misery, of old age, of wickedness and pain, and how unsafe is his own future, [a man] yields to the pessimistic conclusion, cultivates disgust and dread, ceases striving, and finally commits suicide. He thus adds to the mass M of mundane phenomena, independent of his subjectivity, the subjective complement x, which makes of the whole an utterly black picture illumined by no gleam of good. [...] Let it not be said that x is too infinitesimal a component to change the character of the immense whole in which it lies imbedded. Everything depends on the point of view of the philosophic proposition in question," ibid., 531, 529.

29. F. Guattari and G. Deleuze, "The Civilized Capitalist Machine," *Anti-Oedipus*, op. cit., 222. Generally speaking,

readers unfortunately only tend to focus on the critique of psychoanalysis, whereas the authors also develop a theory of debt and money that goes far beyond all the theorizations of these same categories Marxists have come up with.

30. The banking system, credit money, and finance are able to conceal this by converting one flow into another.

31. G. Deleuze, Course of May 28, 1973. http://www.le-terrier.net/deleuze/anti-oedipe1000plateaux/1328-05-73.htm.

32. G. Deleuze, Course of March 7, 1972. http://www.web-deleuze.com/php/texte.php?cle=160&groupe=Anti%20Oedipe%20et%20Mille%20Plateaux&langue=1.

33. Ibid.

34. G. Deleuze, *Nietzsche and Philosophy*, op. cit., 142, 141.

35. F. Nietzsche, *La Genealogy of Morality*, op. cit., 63.

36. G. Deleuze, *Nietzsche and Philosophy*, op. cit., 142.

37. M. Foucault, *Leçons sur la volonté de savoir* (Lectures on the Will to Knowledge) (Paris: Seuil, 2011), 132.

38. Ibid., 128.

39. Ibid.

40. Ibid., 127.

41. G. Deleuze, Course of June 4, 1973. http://www.le-terrier.net/deleuze/anti-oedipe1000plateaux/1404-06-73.htm.

42. Ibid.

43. G. Deleuze, Course of February 22, 1972: "However rich you may be, however great your purchasing power, money as

purchasing power determines a series of powerless signs which receive their power from another flow—financing. And just as money as purchasing power is regulated by the laws of exchange, the other flow is regulated by all the other laws, that is, those of the creation and destruction of money." http://www.le-terrier. net/deleuze/anti-oedipe1000plateaux/1404-06-73.htm.

44. Yet another curiosity! A paper from the Bank for International Settlements (BIS) published by Claudio Borio and Piti Disyatat criticizes US economic leadership for confusing revenue money and capital money. Based on the distinction, they criticize the Federal Reserve's argument, mainly Bernanke's, that the monetary conditions of the crisis are principally the result of easy money, the "global savings glut," which is itself the result of current account balances accumulated by emerging countries (China, above all) and reinvested in the US. The excess savings argument, which relieves European and American banks and monetary authorities of all responsibility, is based on confusion between money as revenue and money as capital. As the authors put it, "The misleading focus on current accounts arguably reflects the failure to distinguish sufficiently clearly between *saving* and *financing*." The first is income not consumed, the second is access to purchasing power. "Investment, and expenditures more generally, require financing, not saving," http://www.bis.org/publ/work346.pdf.

45. F. Guattari and G. Deleuze, *Anti-Oedipus*, op. cit. 228.

46. These remarks on money have a more general significance, since they touch on power relations specific to more than just the economy. The formation of utterances, as in the expression of opinions or communication, does not occur through verbal exchange, which presupposes the equality of speakers (as in Jacques Rancière's theory, for example), but through differentials in flow power. "Power consists precisely in the primacy that superior power flows have over inferior ones. In other words, to conceive of power in terms of exchange and exchange value is as stupid as viewing exchange as the condition for producing speech [...]. It is for this reason that the creation of utterances never works within

an exchange circuit. This is because, in reality, the exchange circuit comes into play or is operative only relative to a circuit of another power, which is itself the circuit of creation/destruction." G. Deleuze, Course of June 4, 1973. Op. cit.

47. F. Guattari and G. Deleuze, *Anti-Oedipus*, op. cit., 197–198.

3. The Ascendency of Debt in Neoliberalism

1. G. Deleuze, "Postscript on Control Societies," *Negotiations, 1972–1990*, op. cit., 81.

2. M. Foucault, *The Birth of Biopolitics*, trans. Graham Burchell (New York: Palgrave Macmillan, 2008), 242.

3. A. Orléan, *Le Pouvoir de la finance* (The Power of Finance) (Paris: Odile Jacob, 1999), 242.

4. "There are three categories of institutional investor: Pension funds, which manage retirement savings in countries where retirement financing is based on a system of capitalization (mainly in the US and UK), mutual funds or investment companies, called SICAVs (open-end collective investment schemes), and insurance companies. The weight of institutional investors in the world economy has become considerable. In late 2006, their total outstanding assets came to around $62 trillion, which exceeded the combined GDP of the largest industrialized nations. That amount should be compared to the approximately $2 trillion in assets China has accumulated through its trade surpluses." E. M. Mouhoud and D. Pilhon, op. cit., 44.

5. A. Orléan, *Le Pouvoir de la finance*, op. cit., 216.

6. E. M. Mouhoud and D. Pilhon, *Le Savoir et la finance*, op. cit., 75.

7. A. Orléan, *Le Pouvoir de la finance*, op. cit., 244.

8. From a review interview in French with Robert Manning, author of *Credit Card Nation* (New York: Basic Books, 2000).

9. Some curious facts about the Greeks. In a business newspaper, uncharacteristically, an article made fun of the rhetoric of "work" espoused in the speeches of both the former French PM, the Socialist Lionel Jospin, and the conservative Sarkozy. The title of the article twists the latter's famous campaign slogan, "Travailler plus pour gagner plus" (Work more to earn more), changing it to "Travailler plus pour... s'endetter plus" (Work more to... earn more debt). Spurred on by Angela Merkel's remark about Greece—"We cannot have a common currency while some have a great deal of vacation time and others very little. In the end, that cannot work"—Philippe Brossard, president of Macrorame, an independent firm for economic and financial research, took a turn at upending clichés about workers, OECD data in hand. The Greeks, it turns out, are the reigning champions of work at 2,119 hours a year. They "work" 52% more than the Germans (1,380 hours). The Greeks also work longer. In Greece, 31% of the population aged 59 to 65 work, compared to 23% in Germany. According to the OECD, labor productivity (GDP output per hour worked) is $34 in Greece, compared to $57 in the US, $55 in France, and $53 in Germany. Although far behind these countries, it is still barely lower than Japan ($38) and higher than Korea ($25). The logical conclusion for the financier: the more you work, the deeper in debt you go. We might call this economic paradox the Salvador-Merkel program, a "double tribute" to our hard-nosed German worker who, trouncing on the southern layabouts, has put us on the right track, and the singer Salvador (Henri, not Dali), who spelled out the program in 1965: "Work is (financial) health. Doing nothing preserves it."

10. "'One in five Americans is unemployed, underemployed or just plain out of work. [...] One in eight Americans is on food stamps. More than 12,000 families are filing for bankruptcy every month. The economic crisis has wiped more than $5 trillion from pensions and savings.' [...] Of course, it's even worse than that [...] with massive budget cuts in education, health

care, and social services in state after state, all across America. At least forty-five states have imposed budget cuts that hurt families and reduce vital services to their most vulnerable residents. Those affected include children, the elderly, the disabled, the sick, the homeless, and the mentally ill, as well as college students and faculty. [...] The devastation is in the details: California is eliminating CalWORKS, a financial assistance program for families in need, a cut that would affect 1.4 million people, two-thirds of whom are children. [...] Maine has cut education grants and funding for homeless shelters. [...] Michigan, Nevada, California, and Utah have eliminated coverage of dental and vision services for those receiving Medicaid. [...] Alabama has canceled services that allow 1,100 seniors to stay in their homes instead of being sent to nursing facilities." A. Huffington, *Third World America: How Our Politicians Are Abandoning the Middle Class and Betraying the American Dream* (New York: Crown, 2011), 4–5, 10, 11.

11. In 2010 the tax cap allowed 925 taxpayers whose inheritance came to more than 16 million euros to receive on average a cut of 381,000 euros from the French government. A law passed in 2007, which, no joke, was supposed to promote work, jobs, and purchasing power, produced instead, in addition to an unprecedented cut in taxes on inheritance and gifts, a whole rhetoric of work only to benefit, in the end, family money.

12. M. Foucault, *Security, Territory, Population*, trans. Graham Burchell (New York: Palgrave Macmillan, 2009), 165.

13. K. Marx, "Comments on James Mill," op. cit., 216.

14. There were two research projects: the first from 2004–2005, whose results were published in *Intermittents et précaires* (Paris: Editions Amsterdam, 2008); the second, part of an initiative uniting scientists and civil society groups in the Île-de-France region, examined different forms of precarious work. Texts from the latter can be found on the CIP website, http://www.cip-idf.org."

15. "[E]valuation presupposes values on the basis of which phenomena are appraised. But, on the other hand and more profoundly, it is values which presuppose evaluations, 'perspectives of appraisal,' from which their own value is derived. The problem of critique is that of the value of values, of the evaluation from which their value arises, thus the problem of their *creation*. Evaluation is defined as the differential element of corresponding values, an element which is both critical and creative. Evaluations, in essence, are not values but ways of being, modes of existence of those who judge and evaluate, serving as principles for the values on the basis of which they judge. This is why we always have the beliefs, feelings and thoughts that we deserve given our way of being or our style of life." G. Deleuze, *Nietzsche and Philosophy*, op. cit., 1.

16. K. Marx, "Comments on James Mill," op. cit., 216.

17. A. Orléan, *Le Pouvoir de la finance*, op. cit., 210.

18. http://www.nanomonde.org/IMG/pdf/lettrefautpaspucer.pdf.

19. See U. Beck, *Risk Society: Towards a New Modernity*, trans. Mark Ritter (London: Sage Publications, 1992).

20. K. Marx, "Comments on James Mill," op. cit., 215.

21. A. J. Haesler, *Sociologie de l'argent et postmodernité*, op. cit., 206.

22. Ibid.

23. G. Deleuze, *Negotiations, 1972–1990*, op. cit., 180.

24. A. J. Haesler, *Sociologie de l'argent et postmodernité*, op. cit., 285.

25. Ibid.

26. F. Guattari and G. Deleuze, *Anti-Oedipus*, op. cit., 235.

27. U. Beck, "Re-Inventing Europe: A Cosmopolitan Vision," in C. Rumford (ed.) *Cosmopolitanism and Europe* (Liverpool: Liverpool University Press, 2007).

28. F. Guattari and G. Deleuze, *Anti-Oedipus*, op. cit., 235.

29. Ibid., 235–236.

30. Ibid., 236.

31. U. Beck, "La société du risque mondialisé" (The Globalized Risk Society), *Le Monde* (March 25, 2011).

32. Ibid.

Conclusion

1. F. Nietzsche, *On the Genealogy of Morality*, op. cit., 62. For an analysis of debt in Kafka's work, see my book *Expérimentations politiques* (Political Experiments) (Paris: Editions Amsterdam, 2009).

Introduction to the Italian Translation

1. *Selected Writings* (New York: Oxford University Press, 2000), 314.

2. Statistics show 14.5% of the population living in poverty, which is already a less than stellar performance. Significantly, the poverty numbers have not decreased with "growth," quite the contrary. This tells us quite a bit about the nature of the supposed growth.

3. Although pensioners represent only 3% of mini-job holders, their numbers are continually on the rise. Totaling 416,000 in 2000, their numbers increased more than 58% in ten years. In 2007, the German government raised the legal retirement age from 65 to 67, whereas the actual age of retirement is 62.1 for men and 61 for women, which entails precarization and a hidden drop in the level of benefits.

4. On January 11, 2012, Destatis published the report "Dark and Bright Spots on the Job Market," in which we learn that "the number of so-called atypical jobs—part-time of less than 20 hours per week, including marginal work, temporary or interim work—rose by 3.5 million from 1991 to 2010, while the number of workers with regular employment dropped by nearly 3.8 million."

5. After moving to a social market economy (ordoliberalism) following the war, social democracy officially converted to neoliberalism on June 1, 2003, when 80% of the German legislature approved Agenda 2010. On June 15, 2003, nearly 90% of Green Party delegates adopted the same program, which established retirement savings accounts, the privatization of public services, etc.

6. The whole of Europe is being forced to follow the American model of deregulated layoffs. The Spanish government approved laws on February 10 that adhere to the same logic: easy layoffs, reductions in wages and unemployment compensation. Unemployment benefits (lasting from 45 to 33 days per year worked) have dropped from a maximum of 42 to 24 months. Layoffs on economic grounds, with benefits (20 days per year worked) set at a 12-month maximum, have been made easier; businesses need only show losses over three consecutive quarters, even if they continue to make profits. Under the same conditions, businesses can unilaterally impose wage cuts and employees may be fired if they refuse them.

7. The "Revenu de solidarité active" (RSA), or Active Solidarity Income, is the French social welfare regime guaranteeing minimum income. Designed to promote "activity," it was implemented on June 1, 2009, replacing the "Revenu minimum d'insertion" (RSI), or Minimum Integration Income, in effect since 1988.—Translator's note.

8. With the RSA, we move from a statutory and institutional logic (equal rights for all!) to a contractual and discretionary logic (each beneficiary must sign a contract preliminary to access to rights) which targets certain labor situations, thus

expanding the overarching aim of social policy: individualization. The "integration" contract is a hybrid of "law" and "contract," which according to Alain Supiot does not establish the equality and autonomy of contracting parties but rather the assertion of an asymmetry of power: "Their aim (with the labor contract) is not to exchange specific goods nor to seal a pact between equals, but to legitimate the exercise of power," since the contracting party is obliged to sign in order to receive benefits. We move from the logic of beneficiary rights to a logic that sets as a condition of welfare a subjective commitment whose foremost requirement is the "work on the self" necessary to make oneself "available" for underemployment and underpaid work. The RSA represents a reversal in the logic of public assistance towards a logic of "debt." It closes once and for all the opening that the RMI had created with regard to the right to social welfare: benefits independent of "employment" that demand nothing directly in return. The RMI maintained, however tenuously, a "national" debt to the "poorest citizens." "During parliamentary debates on the RMI law, despite lingering opposition with regard to the meaning of the contract as well as the adoption of compromise legislation, legislators' desire to end conditions on welfare assistance was completely clear: job market integration was a right and ensuring it was the duty of the institution itself first of all. From the beneficiary's point of view, entry on the job market was a goal not a prerequisite to receiving benefits" (Nicolas Duvoux). The aim of the RSA, on the other hand, is to index benefits to underemployment, availability, employability, and a contract. It institutes not only a poor "worker" but also his guilt, since he is implicitly held to be responsible for his condition and, therefore, to be in debt to society and the State.

semiotext(e) intervention series